REA1
OF T**HE**
KINGDOM
Volume 2

TRADING IN THE HEAVENS

REALMS OF THE KINGDOM

Volume 2

TRADING IN THE HEAVENS

IAN CLAYTON

Edited and produced by Revelation Partners
with grateful thanks to our wonderful transcription team
and other precious Kingdom warriors wishing to
remain anonymous

Ian Clayton: www.sonofthunder.org

Edited and produced by Revelation Partners: www.revelationpartners.org

Published by Son of Thunder Publications:
www.sonofthunderpublications.org

Cover Design by Aspect Reference Design: Caleb.gabrial@clear.net.nz

Graphic Support: Iain Gutteridge iain@ig-graphic-design.co.uk

I.T technical support & media consultants:

Andy Page: gesture2surface@gmail.com

Prav Kumar: pravkmr@yahoo.com

Each chapter in this book is an edited and updated transcript taken from messages given by Ian Clayton at different times over a number of years. There are some minor differences from the audio messages the reader might have listened to before.

ISBN 978-1-911251-02-6

Typeset by Avocet Typeset, Somerton, Somerset TA11 6RT

Printed in the United Kingdom
for Worldwide Distribution

CONTENTS

RECOMMENDATIONS

It is such an honour to be one of those asked to endorse Ian Clayton's new book.

Ian is one of the most loving, grounded and authentic ministers I have ever had the privilege to meet. He is the 'real deal'.

I believe with all my heart that as you read these pages, you will receive a profound, supernatural importation of the Fathers love and intimacy with our beloved, unchanging, majestic, awesome Heavenly Father. The life hanging on the words of each chapter will literally propel its readers into a realm that will change their hearts and intimate relationship with the Father forever.

I walk with my beloved Father in His garden so much. It is my sacred place of meeting with Him; whether it is in the meadows or by the waterfalls of His Eden. Often clinging to Him as a little child would do.

Oh I truly believe beloved, that Ian's books will profoundly change your life and relationship with our most beautiful, incredible, majestic Father of compassion forever.

…And fulfil the eternal cry of His heart…

That we would know Him…

Thank you! Thank you Ian for paying such a price

And for leading us into the sacred holy place of our beautiful Heavenly Father's incredible heart.

Wendy Alec
Founder and Visionary of GOD TV

Through my life with Yehovah I kept hearing a repeated cry from Him. He said, "My sons need to know who they are in relationship with Me."

So many sons struggle with not knowing who they are that it ends up bringing them back to old familiars because they believe this is a safe place; sad but very true.

One day in 2012 I met a man face to face that I knew was the very essence of my Father in the flesh. No it was not Yeshua but Ian Clayton.

Ian has been one of the single most important influences in my spiritual life. Yes, I am fortunate to know him.

A unique assignment on Ian during this season is these books. There are plenty of books on growth in Father's Heaven coming out, but none have this consistent, everlasting fruit within them.

You can read a portion of his book today, and next year when you read it a different level will be ignited within you to grow.

Ian's book is everlasting fruit in living word form.

Ian is like placing a dose of massive fertilizer on your life that never stops till you reach fullness in that certain area of your life.

Ian's books will bring sons out of the old way of thinking. Thank you Abba Father!

Our next step is living in the best everlasting life Yehovah has always planned for each one of His sons. This book is a great start to your true life in revealing your destiny scroll.

Bless you Ian and your family for this great wealth given to the sons of Melchizedek!

I honor you! Your platform is my springboard. All students are to surpass their teachers. What a way to live in this multiverse of my Father's Kingdom.

To Infinity and beyond!

Kathy Madden
Heavens Call
Creative Blue Light Beings

We're so happy to recommend this second volume to anyone seeking a deeper relationship with the Father. We love how Ian teaches from his experience but then gives practical tips and exercises to help believers engage in days and weeks the same pathways Ian spent months and years discovering for himself. We love Ian's heart to share these Kingdom dynamics to help raise up a generation of sons, lovers and glory dwellers manifesting the supernatural ways and lifestyle of Heaven on earth.

We believe you will find this second volume, as the first volume, a great aid in your own journey of seeing the Father face to face and walking in the true ways that the Father always intended for you to walk.

Many blessings
Matthew and Pearl Nagy
Glory Company

It's a great honour and huge privilege to recommend this exciting new book from Ian Clayton to anyone who has a desire to mature and learn how to walk more fully in their God given destiny as manifest sons. Realms of the Kingdom Volume 2 Trading in the Heavens, just like volume 1, is packed full of priceless wisdom and insight which will help you practically outwork your scroll and enable you to take back all that has been stolen from you by the enemy.

There is an army of mature sons that God is raising up in these days and I believe that Ian Clayton is at the forefront of that army. These teachings in this volume, and volume 1, are not just teachings to give knowledge but are revelations from the Holy Spirit that will help train and transform this army into governmental mature sons, who learn how to live in the realm of the Kingdom of the Father, beyond the veil and from that realm begin to respond to creations cry and rule and reign as kings and priests in the order of Melchizedek – and would you believe it, that is just beginning!

Stephen Mckie
scotlandablaze.com

What a privilege to write about a mentor and friend, Ian Clayton. His words 'this is normal,' opened up a world to me that I had kept quiet about all my life.

I want to honour his wife and family for lending him to us and am so very grateful for his inter action with my family and his fathering of my children in their times of need.

His books have become 'life handbooks' for hundreds of people around the world and I am so excited for the release of Volume Two.

As you study and engage with what he shares in this volume, may it engage with you and release the mysteries of the Kingdom Realms to you in a profound way.

I honour you Ian and am grateful for your dedication to the truth being revealed.

Lindi Masters
Ignite Hubs International

ACKNOWLEDGEMENTS

Collaborating with Ian Clayton to write this second volume of his revelatory teaching has been an honour and a privilege. Thank You Papa YHVH, Your ongoing commission to see these books written has been a strength and an inspiration to us, with visionary experiences of arenas of Heaven and the angelic amid the battles.

Recording prophecy and inspirational teaching has always been our heart passion, but there has never been a speaker whose words have inspired us in the creation of a book until Ian Clayton was invited to Wales a number of years ago. Our thanks and tribute go to Justin Abraham and COBH community for their pioneering walk, pushing through the religious constraints we knew, to find a new level of victory through intimacy with Yeshua and experience of functioning from heavenly realms. Our greatest goal in seeing Ian Clayton's work published, is to unlock the experience of this reality for those wanting to find it.

We want to honour the support, friendship and dedication of our IT and media team and the many others whose attention and diligence have been invaluable, together with the graphic design expertise of several talented team members, especially our design lead Gabrial Heath of Aspect Reference Design, who created the cover for us and Iain Gutteridge for his excellent graphic support throughout. We owe a special gratitude to our media and IT support team, including Andy Page who created the YouTube video, Prav Kumar who created much of the website and our spectacular project manager and 'go to guy' who wishes to remain anonymous.

We want to especially thank all the Kingdom family in Christ who donated to help with the creation and publication costs of this book, we couldn't have done it without your touching generosity and we were moved and encouraged by all the wonderful messages of support, thank you so much.

Our special thanks goes to our wonderful, international transcription team, whose generous and loving companionship on the journey brought about the birth of this second book months before it might otherwise have been available. Thank you so much, all of you, our friends named and those wishing to remain anonymous. May the Lord pour the blessing your work gives to others into your hearts and lives as well.

We cannot give adequate thanks to the numerous precious sisters and several dedicated brothers who walked with us along the journey of creating this book, including proof readers, intercessors and friends of wise counsel, without whom this book would still be a vision. They have chosen to remain anonymous but they continue to be counted with affection as part of the Revelation Partners family.

We also want to express our love and gratitude for the kindness, encouragement and prayer of many which opened doors along the way, including Stephen McKie of Scotland Ablaze; Matthew and Pearl Nagy of Glory Company and the wonderful Kingdom family in Horsham; Liz Wright, Lulu, Ann, Anne, Funmi and precious prayer community in Guildford and faithful intercessors and friends Michelle Beare and Michelle Kerslake – thank you so much for your loving support for this work as we walk into heavenly realms together.

Finally, we want to express our affection and gratitude to Ian, his wife, family and team, especially Karl Whitehead, for their wisdom, support and oversight of this labour of love.

Revelation Partners
United Kingdom
2016

Chapter 1

Unlocking your Scroll of Destiny

For us to understand where we are going and what YHVH[1] wants us to do, we have to understand and remember where we have come from. We have got to go back to the very root of our origins, to the source of our life and how we were originally created and made as a spirit being so that we can understand the call and mandate of YHVH that is on each one of us.

In the Bible it says,

"Before I formed you in the womb I knew you.
before you were born I sanctified you;
I ordained you a prophet to the nations" (Jeremiah 1:5).

The "Yasod" is the governing bench of three as well as the council of YHVH. In the beginning YHVH sat as the bench of three in His council and from under the shepherd's rod Jeremiah received the scroll of records for his life. It was from this arena and from this governmental bench that Jeremiah was ordained to bear out his scroll on the face of the earth. In the very beginning YHVH provided the source of everything for Jeremiah, when he was released to come to the earth, from within the relationship of YHVH.

YHVH sets in place and ordains your walk to fulfil a mandate that you agreed with Him before coming to live in this Adamic

---

[1] Many of the references to God throughout this book have been changed where appropriate, to the four letters in the Hebrew alphabet that the original Hebrew text of the Bible uses to reference the name of our God, often transliterated as Yahweh.

form. Your mission and reason for coming to the earth was to fulfil that mandate. YHVH has a plan to unfold for your life, but our big problem is that we have amnesia about what that plan was.

We get amnesia by the encasing of our spirit man by our physical body and our soul, then by retraining our records of the memory of Heaven by overlaying them with the knowledge gleaned and framed by the physical world we live in. So we lose the memory of what we came out of and what we were called to do.

Life from Conception

I want to describe what happens at the point our life begins, when a man and a woman come together and the seed from the man joins the egg from the woman. From this you get the forming of a woven fabric and foundation of a covenant going through a protocoled agreement system, deciding things like being 'big' or 'small', 'short' or 'tall', 'brown eyes' or 'blue eyes', 'bald head' or 'lots of hair', 'big nose' or 'small nose'. You can see the assembling of this agreement between the two seeds under an electron microscope. This is the point that every single protocol for your life begins. It only takes about three or four seconds. The moment it does that and comes together completed, there is a flash of light on the outside of that single cell that can be seen with the electron microscope. Scientists call it energy. I want to reframe it completely differently and call it the opening of the realm of eternity to make a way for your spirit man to arrive. That flash of light is the arc of Heaven between the ovaries over the seat of the womb.

"And they shall make an ark of acacia wood... And you shall overlay it with pure gold, inside and out... And you shall put into the ark the Testimony which I will give you. "You shall make a mercy seat of pure gold... And you shall make two cherubim of gold; of hammered work you shall make them at the two ends of the mercy seat... And the cherubim shall stretch out their wings above, covering the mercy seat with their wings, and they shall face one another; the faces of the cherubim shall be toward the mercy seat... And there I will meet with you, and I will speak with you from above the mercy seat, from between the two cherubim which are on the ark of the Testimony" (Exodus 25:10-11, 16-18, 20, 22).

The ark of the covenant has two cherubim on it. The High Priest would go into the Holy of Holies and sing and intone the names of YHVH. This would produce resonance and vibration inside the ark, which would then set up a frequency as a super conductor of power. The frequency would activate the ark, which would vibrate, creating energy. Power from the vibrational frequency would create a release of physical power to form an arc of light that would go from wingtip to wingtip between the two top wings of the cherubim. That arc of light was an opening and a window into the Kingdom realm so that the realm of Heaven would open and the presence of YHVH could come through that window and sit on the mercy seat.

A woman has two ovaries that do a similar thing in my opinion. The womb is the seat prepared for the spirit being that comes out of the realm of eternity. An arc is formed between the two ovaries, which creates the open window for the spirit being to come through into the womb when the two seeds join together. The scientists call it energy. I call it the Lord's way of opening a window where the spirit Kingdom realm opens up and the spirit being comes out of the realm of eternity and goes into the womb. To me that is an amazing thing.

You and I come out of the realm of eternity with our testimony scroll. This is now wrapped and sealed inside your spirit man. The instant your physical body starts to form it starts making a place for your spirit man to live in.

So we come out of Heaven as a spirit being and start living inside the womb of a woman. It was amazing and freaky for me personally that I knew very quickly after my wife became pregnant, because I was aware of other things going on within her body and because I was aware that there was another spirit being sitting inside her that was another entity born out of Heaven.

Now we can focus on what begins to happen here. You came out of the realm of eternity, a realm of pure white light with the full knowledge of all you knew of YHVH and go into the womb of a woman. Your spirit being has the full knowledge of YHVH and all of the realm of eternity. Your spirit man came out of that realm with full knowledge and an agreement to complete a work down here. Your spirit man's objective is to take that record back, completed on the earth, as a testimony and witness to Heaven.

You are born from the realm of creative light into darkness, to see the light, to reflect the light, to become light once again.

What begins to happen in the womb of a mother, that little single cell, that has come together in genetic covenant begins to multiply. There is a dividing, replicating process that begins. It begins to replicate that original cell created from the joining together of your mother and father's DNA. It begins to multiply itself until it gets this little ball of cells. The original cell formed from the joining of your parent's DNA, which is what you are made in the record of, carries that record to complete your physical body.

That original cell implodes into the centre of the conglomeration of cells and starts to form the human heart. Your heart is made from the original cell created at the covenantal joining of your mother and father's seed, which is the record of your earthly testimony. That is why as a man thinks in his heart so he is, (Proverbs 23:7) because whatever your parents thought about, looked at and experienced in every form, is now in the record of the very cells of your body. Your heart is also the house of your soul. Your soul came out of the fusion of your spirit being to the physical form of human DNA and is formed as the mediator for your spirit to be able to engage the realm of physical creation. Originally you were created as a spirit being that has a soul and lives in a physical world. The only reason you have a physical body is so that your spirit man can interact with the physical world.

What happens now is that those cells begin to multiply. The first thing that begins to form is the human skull and the backbone. The little baby's body at this stage looks something like the form of a tadpole. The key issue and question here is, what is the human DNA doing when it is forming that body? I believe its first requirement is making a house for your spirit man to live in and weaving it around the human spirit that now lives inside the womb of the woman. The physical body has now become a temple inside the womb of a woman for the spirit being to live in.

This is the first house that is made. This again is where your spirit man lives and has its existence within that cavity of your skull and down your spinal column. No blood penetrates this area of the physical body. There is a membrane that separates it called the blood brain barrier. Even UV radiation will not penetrate through that membrane. What happens is that your spirit man gets a house built for it to live in by your DNA and your human body forms around that.

Our Conflicting Testimony Scrolls

Now here is the central and core problem with our current form: I, as a spirit being have come out of the realm of eternity with a testimony scroll, a witness in Heaven and the full knowledge of Heaven. I have also come out of the realm of eternity with full knowledge of what I am going to do on the face of the earth, bearing YHVH's image. My issue is that my parent's DNA has a different testimony scroll, which has been formed in their image, in their brokenness, in their memories and their recall. This DNA forms a different scroll that wraps around that spirit scroll and begins to shut the spirit man's record down. I then get born and I come out of the womb of the woman and my problems start to worsen, due to the pre-programming of my physical form and my accumulating of human memories in created light framing the physical world around me.

Just an amazing thing to note about Mary, as a virgin, is that she still had a part of her body that had not been broken through sexual union. Jesus came through the matrix of her virginity and broke into the world through a blood covenant in His mother's womb. So He was crowned with a blood covenant.

We have this human body that wraps around our spirit being. When you come out of the womb you begin to get taught to live from the outside in. All through your childhood you are learning from the outside in. You are learning the protocols of how to see. When a child first sees it does not see out there in the physical world. It sees inside its brain on the screen of its mind (we still do in fact), until the child learns that what it is seeing inside its brain is out there. The child does this by learning how to create memory from the accumulation of its world being framed around it by measuring distance with its visual and touch senses. If you have ever watched a new born baby, it looks with this weird, wide eyed expression. I have watched all three of my children go through this weird, wide eye experience. Remember, you do not see with your eyes, you see through them.

A child gets its hand and it will reach out, trying to figure out what it is seeing inside its head and how far away what it is seeing is. It measures this in memory inside its brain, forming neuron trees until it learns, through the repetitive learning processes and protocols, measuring each present experience against the past. These become memories, meaning that each time it touches something, new created memory is accumulated measuring and creating its understanding of the physical environment around it.

Then, within about three weeks, the child can see something like twenty-four inches. That is why it can see its dad's face and begins to respond accordingly to a greater range of environments. The child begins to learn that everything coming from the outside is now its reality, and in turn begins to shut down the testimony and remembrance of what it was in Heaven before being on the earth and the memory of what it knew on the inside. This comes about by the formation of new neuron pathways. Doing this shuts down the witness and record of what it came out of Heaven with and it shuts down the voice of the record of its scroll by the present that it now lives in. The record of the scroll that speaks inside of you gets shuts down. So gradually, all the information that is supposed to be flowing from the inside out gets shut down because you learn and are taught to flow from the outside in.

We grow up learning all this from the outside in until the memory is no longer active within us of how to live from the inside out.

Then we get born again and have an instant and fairly major problem because our outside body has been dictating to us how to live, having all its needs being met, and not necessarily in the right way, by the soul mediating its desire. We get born again and suddenly our spirit man is empowered to actually begin to stand up and take the reins of influence back. Our biggest issue now is that there is another scroll sitting on the outside called your soul and body that will fight for its position and will say, "No you won't. I want control. I have had control all through this life so far. I won't give up easily." Just because you have been born again does not mean your spirit gets to be in charge. You can just stay locked up in there, because your body and soul will want to stay in charge and stay in control. Your body and soul will fight against the revelation of Jesus within you. That is why we have to crucify ourselves daily, which is not an easy task but one that can be accomplished. We have already looked at dividing soul and spirit in Realms of the Kingdom Volume 1.

Moving forward, we are birthed out of the realm of the eternal presence of YHVH with five things. It can be closely connected to and pictured like a hand but is in fact more like a tree that provides the covering for a fruitful life.

Part of our engagement with the presence of YHVH is understanding some of these things, so that the realm of the Kingdom can actually manifest itself through us. We have a testimony scroll that we need to unravel. The only way to unravel it is to present yourself as a living sacrifice by opening up your inner life parts and exposing them to the presence of Jesus as our High Priest.

The reason you need to expose the inner parts of your life to Him on the inside is because He needs our surrender. When the high priest used to cut and prepare the sheep for sacrifice, he would open it up, cut it in half and open the two halves up. What it was symbolizing was the exposing of the full testimony of its life, uncovered and completely vulnerable. So what YHVH is wanting us to do is to open ourselves up so that the full testimony of what He has written for us to do can be exposed, uncovered, become unlocked and be able to be read, seen, decreed and begin to manifest again. This scroll will attest and speak of itself, of as it is in Heaven, so that all we have come out of Heaven to do will be seen on the earth.

The thing I love about science is that it backs up everything YHVH has established. When you come out of the realm of Heaven and out of the realm of eternity, you are created as an eternal spirit being. Your spirit man comes out of that realm of eternity, comes into your mother's womb, and the moment your spirit being touches the cell of the DNA, the human soul gets formed. That is the life of YHVH engaging the seed that releases the nature of the soul to be formed because the spirit man brings that breath of life with it.

Creative Light and Created Light

There are two completely different sources of light: creative light and created light. The first thing you come out of the realm of eternity with when you are released is creative light. You are a creative light being. You are a spirit being that carries the full capacity of the creative light of YHVH. Creative light is what happened when YHVH said, "Let there be light" (Genesis 1:3). Created light is when He put the sun in place to shine with its light. This will be discussed in future books in much more detail.

When you take a light beam and shine it into a prism, it shatters into seven spectrums of light we call the rainbow. When you and I came out of the realm of eternity we came out reflecting the spectrum of the realm of eternity – creative light, pure and white. However, when we entered into the womb, you and I came into the realm of created light. At this point we begin to take on the nature of the fallen measure of light described as created light, still white but from a different source. Because of this, our eternal light spectrum shatters and breaks into the seven created colours of the rainbow.

All the different spectrums of light that are in the physical world around us are amazing. A scientific fact for you: if you take the colours of the rainbow and put them on a keyboard as seven keys, and if you were to take every other spectrum of light that is currently visible, not just to human beings, such as ultra violet, infra-red etc that are in creation and put them all on the same keyboard, the keyboard would physically reach from the earth to the moon.

It is amazing when you take the seven colours of the rainbow, they will go back into the source, which is white light. We are supposed to be transformed back into the original pattern as white light beings, completely reflecting the glory of YHVH. That is how we were originally created. You come out of the realm of eternity as light because you are a light being from the realm of eternity. The Bible says that YHVH is light (1 John 1:5). You come out of the womb of the presence and the person of YHVH into creation bearing the full record of that light.

Fragrance

The second thing you come out of the realm of eternity with is fragrance. Fragrances are very interesting things. Fragrances are actually a vibration that is picked up by your nose hairs. Scripture says, to YHVH we are the fragrance of Christ (2 Corinthians 2:15).

When the Bible talks about anointing with oil (the fragrances of YHVH), it does not mean the religious practice of putting a drop on your finger and putting it on the middle of someone's forehead while making the sign of the cross and saying, "I anoint you with oil today". That is not what anointing with oil really means. To understand the anointing with oil process, you have to go back into the Old Testament where the priest or prophet used to anoint someone with oil. They would take a horn of oil. On the top of the horn of oil there was a wax plug. As the prophet prayed and held the horn over the person's head, if that was the person that was chosen by YHVH then he would witness this by the dancing fire on their heads. This in turn would melt the wax plug, and the whole horn of oil would run out over them.

"Now the LORD said to Samuel... "Fill your horn with oil, and go; I am sending you to Jesse the Bethlehemite. For I have provided Myself a king among his sons."

Jesse made seven of his sons pass before Samuel. And Samuel said to Jesse, "The LORD has not chosen these." And Samuel said to Jesse, "Are all the young men here?"

Then he said, "There remains yet the youngest, and there he is, keeping the sheep."

And Samuel said to Jesse, "Send and bring him. For we will not sit down till he comes here." So he sent and brought him in. Now he was ruddy, with bright eyes, and good-looking.

And the LORD said, "Arise, anoint him; for this is the one!" Then Samuel took the horn of oil and anointed him in the midst of his brothers; and the Spirit of the LORD came upon David from that day forward" (1 Samuel 16:1, 10-13).

Samuel came to all of Jesse's sons and, until he found the last one, nothing happened. They then called David, this young man way out in the dessert tending and living with the sheep, who seemed too ruddy, not tall or strong. In fact, he was just a young teenage boy who had been taking lambs out of the mouths of lions and bears and killing them; he looked immaterial in his outside appearance but his heart was already fully connected to YHVH. Samuel gets his horn of oil and puts it over the head of David. The wax plug melts and the oil comes out of the horn.

Oil carries frequency in it. Pure oil has measures of frequency inside it that affect the human body. Jesus was given gold (the balm of Gilead), frankincense and myrrh. Frankincense has one of the highest frequencies of any naturally occurring oil in its pure form. This has a resonant frequency that can help tremendously with your health and well-being especially with your physical body. In those days they did not have antibiotics. They had fragrant oil and blends that were used to help in the arenas of medicine. So when the Bible says, *"Is anyone among you sick? Let him call for the elders of the church, and let them pray over him, anointing him with oil…"* (James 5:14), it actually means to pour oil all over you and to pray.

Fragrances are so interesting. When you smell a fragrance your brain assimilates the vibration of the fragrance and you associate the smell with a word, usually taught by your parents as a baby. When your nose hairs pick up the vibration, translated as the smell, the small hairs in your nose do not actually register the smell, they pick up the frequency and vibration, triggering the memory connected to the vibration as a smell. Your nose hairs, not your brain, translate that as scent.

In the desert certain cactus flowers smell like rotten meat! When the cactus flower produces the smell it comes out in the form of a vapour that can be detected by infra-red light, which is the way many insects see and is attractive to flies. For them that frequency and colour means it is something good for them to eat. So they go to it, but the key is the smell, which attracts the flies so they can pollinate the flower because there are no bees in the desert.

If you have other things attached to your life, emitting their own fragrance, this fragrance will attract to you whatever recognises it as their home. We are supposed to be the fragrance of YHVH in Christ Jesus – being attractive to YHVH and the angelic realm.

"Now thanks be to God who always leads us in triumph in Christ, and through us diffuses the fragrance of His knowledge in every place. For we are to God the fragrance of Christ among those who are being saved and among those who are perishing" (2 Corinthians 2:14-15).

If you are not carrying the fragrance of Jesus Christ and the evidence of the platform of what He is doing inside your life, then you are going to be attracting something else to your life. What I have found is that demonic spirit forces feed into the source of corrupt fragrances and live in the product of the fragrance inside our lives.

Our Song

The third thing you come out of eternity with is a song. Everyone's individual DNA vibrates and each person's vibration has a different sound and tone or a song that is released around them. Scientists can quantum-physically take your DNA, put it into a milli-voltmeter and measure and read the frequency and the sound of your DNA that sings an individual song. This is usually an expression of worship to the presence of YHVH. That is why we are the song of the Lord. It is our DNA that is vibrating and singing a song that desires to be released.

"I am confident and unafraid;
for Yah ADONAI is my strength and my song,
and he has become my salvation!" (Isaiah 12:2 CJB).

The problem is that if our DNA is messed up and there is something else sitting inside it, then we are going to be singing a different song that is out of harmony with the sound of Heaven. That will then be attracting things that live outside of the harmony of Heaven. To get our body back into alignment is to come back into the realm of the presence of YHVH so that our song is sung unto the Lord. That is what the Bible says, *"...In psalms and hymns and spiritual songs, singing and making melody in your heart to the Lord"* (Ephesians 5:19). It is the sound of who you are coming as an offering and a fragrance before the presence of YHVH, having the original seed the heart reformed and reframed to sound like Him.

Our Equation

The fourth thing you come out of the realm of Heaven with is a mathematical equation. Our body can be mathematically calculated. How do we know YHVH is a mathematician? The Hebrew language itself is a mathematical equation. If you do not know, you need to go and do some study on linguistic mathematics. You will find that the Bible is actually perfect. They have studied it with computer binomials and it is actually perfect. It is amazing when you get the original Hebrew language and can put it into a special computer programme. It is just unbelievable what comes out. It makes your brain fry. The Word of YHVH has been written by many different people over thousands of years but it all matches perfectly mathematically. That is YHVH all over.

You come out of the realm of eternity with a mathematical formula because in created light, for a solid object to form there must be a mathematical formula to measure created interference. Your mathematical formula forms you as a solid being in created light. It is this mathematical formula that makes you a solid being.

Quantum physically you actually measure as 99.9% empty space, which effectively makes us all holograms. So quantum physically you are just a hologram. You are just an empty shell that vibrates with a mathematical formula in created light that moves at 197,272 miles per second. To understand and have some idea of how fast created light travels, if I were to hold a gun and shoot the gun, bang, the bullet will be able to cover the entire circumference of the world twice, by the time I take my finger off the trigger.

A mathematical equation interferes with the frequency of created light, causing it to form a solid object. That is why the created world around us is not made of solid objects, it does not exist in the way we think. It is 99.9% empty space. It is just an observed, mathematical formula in created light. If I am a creative light being then this world is subject to me as I was made before it was.

It is important for us to understand that YHVH has set things in place for us to see His kingdom come. Science and the Kingdom should never have been separated. All Quantum physics does is back up the reality of the Kingdom.

Our Destiny Scroll

The fifth thing you come out of eternity with is your testimony scroll. In the Bible it says, *"They overcame him by the blood of the Lamb and by the word of their testimony..."* (Revelation 12:11). Unfortunately, we have been taught that our testimony is what YHVH has delivered us from, and what has happened in our lives along the journey of getting saved, changed and transformed to where I am today. This to me is my witness, the things I have accomplished. That does not empower you to overcome. What empowers you to overcome is doing what you were designed to do and what you came out of Heaven with which is called your 'Testimony Scroll'. Your scroll comes out of the realm of the Kingdom with all the protocols of your function recorded on it, to walk on the face of the earth in this day. That is how you will overcome the enemy. When you walk you will display the measure of the glory of YHVH that was written and agreed about before you were on the earth. Again this will only come about as it is unlocked inside of you as you walk through becoming a living sacrifice.

> *David says, "My frame was not hidden from You,*
> *When I was made in secret,*
> *And skillfully wrought in the lowest parts of the earth.*
> *Your eyes saw my substance, being yet unformed.*
> *And in Your book they all were written,*
> *The days fashioned for me,*
> *When as yet there were none of them"* (Psalm 139:15-16).

Somehow David knew about this, because David had the capacity to live out of the future in his day. You see, the key of David is living out of the supply of the future. If you are living out of the future the present cannot harm you. He said things like, *"Do not take Your Holy Spirit from me"* (Psalm 51:11), when the Holy Spirit was not even given yet (John 7:39).

We come out with things written on our testimony scroll that

27

have become a mystery. The only one that could do those things written on your scroll is you. Just because you are doing good things does not mean to say that they are on your testimony scroll. You only get rewarded for what you are doing on your testimony scroll, for doing His will, which is the outworking of your scroll, not for good works.

That is why the Bible says, *"Not every one that says unto me, Lord, Lord, shall enter into the kingdom of heaven; but he that does the will of my Father who is in heaven. Many will say to me in that day, Lord, Lord, have we not prophesied in your name? and in your name have cast out demons? and in your name done many wonderful works? And then will I profess unto them, I never knew you: depart from me, you that work iniquity"* (Matthew 7:21-23 KJ2000).

The word iniquity means doer of your own thing. Actually, what it really means is whatever the eye is hooked into multiples. If we have been busy doing our own thing, our eyes have been hooked into something that was not on our testimony scroll. A favourite saying of mine is, "it does not amount to a hill of beans" actually to the presence of YHVH. What iniquity means is that you did not know Him. Remember you are there when you are here. So YHVH wants us to get to know Him here, as it was there, because YHVH wants to take us back there, to where we have come from with the full knowledge of our scroll.

Hebraically, Hebrews always think in a circular way. Linear thinking is Greek. Greek thinking goes $1+2+3=6$. Hebrew thinking goes $1+2+3=6=3+2+1$ because the end must always equal the beginning. You find the basic law is that the end must equal the beginning. It is the law of first mention and the law of last mention coming together to form the realm of eternity, which is circular. For Hebrews the tree of the knowledge of good and evil is something that unravels completion and the tree of life is something that brings to completion. Many of us have been fed by the tree of the knowledge of good and evil by being taught linear thinking, which does not come to completion. It stops half way in the middle. The whole education system is based on linear thinking, which produces death. It does not produce Kingdom life.

In schools we read from left to right. Hebrews read differently to us. They do not read from left to right, they read from right to left. Hebrews are taught to think right to left, not left to right. We write from left to right but they write from right to left. When they read a scroll, they open and then they read that part. They hallow the Word of YHVH, so will not expose all of it at once. They will read a piece and then seal it up and open it up at another piece until the scroll is finished.

Wanting to know the whole now is very much the way of Greek thinking – reading the end of a book before the beginning. Hebraic thinking means you open up the portion and you fulfil the portion that has been assigned to you in that season. This prepares and empowers you for the next season once this piece has been sealed and is now done. This enables you to open up another piece. One of the issues we face is in the Greek way of thinking and the way we have been taught. We have been taught to want everything and to want it now. Unfortunately, what that does is it keeps us immature and having no responsibility. To a Hebrew, opening the whole book exposes the full testimony, causing our bombardment and a lack of maturity and witness because it is not manifested, revealed or even understood.

Regarding the unwrapping of your scroll, the Father wants to give us a little piece to see if we will be faithful with a little. This He does so He can open up a little bit more for us. When we are faithful with what he has given, He will give us a bit more, until the whole scroll begins to get unravelled and the truth of that begins to sound inside of us.

Scrolls are really interesting in the Kingdom spirit realm. In the mountain of YHVH there is a scroll room and you can go and get information on every single thing ever created and how it was done from there. The scrolls are fascinating; the words on them are written in what appears to be Hebraic writing. When engaging these scrolls, each letter and word will come off the page and form a door that leads into revelation about the testimony of that word, its function and how it is mandated to operate in the world and in Heaven. You can only live in the word when you go into the door opened by the letters. It is not reading as we would read on a piece of paper. An example is: "And Ian went down the road." The 'And' comes off the page, displays and opens up and reveals a picture to you. 'Went' comes off the page and does the same thing. Each picture is a doorway of entry into revelation for the fullness of that to manifest and be revealed. When you begin to open your scroll you will find that it will behave in exactly the same way because it is a living thing. As you walk it out, it will reveal your life's purpose and will help you to begin to remember what your call was from the very beginning.

YHVH wants us to live out of the revelation of our scroll. He does not want us to live by bread alone but by every Word that proceeds out of His mouth. This helps to release the testimony of YHVH because this scroll of ours must have a voice and must speak. When our scroll speaks here on earth, it will speak and bear witness there in Heaven. You will then find that the scroll manifests down here on earth. When both up there and down here are saying the same thing, this will form an image and a shadow on the earth of 'as it is in Heaven'. This in turn will release an attestation and a descending of Heaven to earth to frame itself in its own image, now being released on the earth.

Activation

Let's have communion – Thank you Jesus.

Father, we want to thank You that You sent Your Son onto the earth, to give us a record of Your DNA. Father, I thank You that You overshadowed Mary and You implanted the Yod chromosome into the womb of Mary's body and You took on the nature of man, carrying the glory and the fullness of YHVH, in that one piece of the twenty three chromosomes.

Lord, I want to thank You that You came to earth to give us that record to birth it in Mary to give us the establishment of a new protocol that our body could get changed into, to give us a record to engage inside of us.

Lord, I want to thank you that your body carries the testimony of the resurrection on the mountain, of being transfigured in the glory of the sound, the frequency and the wave of your manifestation as a fullness of a son.

Lord, I want to thank You that you have given us this testimony in the physical form of your body.

Lord, You said, *"Whoever eats My flesh and drinks My blood has eternal life..."* (John 6:54).

Lord, this is life in its fullness, in the realm of eternity here today, on the face of the earth, characterised in these symbols that we hold in our hand today.

We want to acknowledge the importance of these symbols of death, resurrection, burial and everything associated with Your Son. We want to acknowledge the healing power that is in the restoring glory, that You gave us in the record to fully restore, fully heal and fully bring to manifestation.

Father, today we receive this as sons, we receive it with full knowledge. We take it willingly in the name of Yeshua. Lord, we speak the life of YHVH into this today. We release the life and call it into its being, call it into its fullness as a testimony on earth, as a symbol Lord. Lord, this is not who You are but as a symbol of what You gave us and we acknowledge this symbol today, by faith, in Jesus' name we eat today. (Let us eat and drink. I want you to put your hands on your stomach).

Father, today by faith I engage the sound of Your resurrection. Father, I engage it inside of me and I draw it into the sound of my DNA. I draw it into my body, the sound of the frequency of the light of YHVH and the glory on the mountain of YHVH. I draw it into my physical body today out of what I have inside of me in the name of Yeshua HaMashia.

Father, today I draw on the record of the testimony of Your DNA that I now have in my physical body. Father, I draw it and I command it to go into my bones, into the marrow of my bones that my bones may take on the image of Your presence and that my DNA would be changed to carry the similitude of who You are as it is in Heaven Father.

Lord, today I speak to my bones and I command them to live, that the breath of YHVH would breathe into them, and that which is within me would come back to the truth of the life I was really given, not this life that I live in today. Lord, I engage this freely, I release it to flow through me and out of me, to change me into

Your image, for it is written, that *"As we have borne the image of the man of dust, we shall also bear the image of the heavenly Man"* (1 Corinthians 15:49).

Father, today I want to thank You for that realm of Your Kingdom that gets unlocked within me, to flow from within me to change my spirit, to transform my soul and to transfigure my body, in the name of Yeshua MaHashiach.

Father, today I want to bless these people, that You would be their shade upon their right hand, that the sun would not smite them by day, nor the moon by night. Lord, preserve them from all evil, preserve their going in and their coming forth, this time forward and even for evermore.

Father, let the light of Your presence shine upon them and let the countenance of Your glory be seen in them, and around them. Father, lead them into paths of righteousness, that the Word of YHVH would direct their path, that the Word would make the path before them plain, because their steps would be ordered by the Lord.

Father, I bless them today with the knowledge of the Kingdom, and the impartation and release of Your Kingdom, that as they sit and as they meditate and as they engage and as they practise that You would truly draw them into sonship reality.

Father, I ask that the blessing of YHVH would begin to sit like a shadow and a covering over these people, that the manifestation of the huppah of YHVH (Joel 2:16), would engage them and become a covering of blessing for them.

Lord we bless the readers in the name of Jesus Christ.

Amen. Hallelujah!

CHAPTER 2

COVENANTS OF GOD

Jesus Christ wants to do something that is going to change us and affect our lives for eternity. Everything we do today is a dressing room for tomorrow and YHVH is going to enable us to come to Him and receive from Him so that when we do come there we are already clothed in His likeness. YHVH wants to engage us more than we want to engage Him. He wants to get hold of us and shake us so that we can begin to stand underneath the anointing that He needs to be released into our communities *"…Those things that can be shaken will be removed and taken away, namely, the first creation. As a result, those things that remain cannot be shaken"* (Hebrews 12:27 VOICE).

Holy Spirit will not come to an unpurified vessel, but He will flow through a sanctified vessel. That means someone that was so full of garbage in their life but brought it under the anointing, under the government and under the Lordship of Jesus Christ, and from there He says, "Now I have got a vessel." Many people say that YHVH is going to come and give us new wineskins. That is not actually what the Bible says. The Greek word that is used for new wine skin by Paul in the Bible is "ἀνακαινόω" (Strong's 341) transliterated as "anakainoó" which means "made new again". YHVH is not going to give you a new wineskin, He is going to make *you* new again. There are some things that YHVH has given us in the Word that we need to learn how to use to anakainoó ourselves.

In this chapter I am going to teach on a subject that I have found to be a fundamental foundation in my life, to be able to access the realm of the Kingdom and walk with the presence of YHVH, experiencing Him in a very real way: covenants of YHVH. The Bible says, *"My people are destroyed for lack of knowledge..."* (Hosea 4:6). It is that lack of knowledge that robs us of the inheritance that YHVH has for us in these covenants, so I want to just lay some things out that we need to understand and because they are weapons of war against the enemy. YHVH wants to use these covenants around our lives to facilitate His move in us and through us.

The covenant of adoption has been included in Realms of the Kingdom Volume 1 in the Gateways and Seven Spirits of YHVH chapters. I want to look at the covenant of promise and the covenant of the blood of Jesus in this chapter.

A covenant is a binding agreement between two parties. The closest thing that we have today to this understanding is the covenant of marriage. In Old Testament times a covenant was far more in depth than ours are today. Usually there was an exchange made from one to the other, a promise made or something that was given. Jesus Christ was the supreme sacrifice that sealed our position as heirs to the throne and the Kingdom of YHVH.

From a Hebrew perspective a covenant says, "Everything I have that belongs to me and is at my personal disposal is yours and is at your disposal when I sign that document. So when you get attacked I will come and rescue you and help you fight; when you go through hell, I will walk through hell with you; when you walk on the mountain tops and rejoice I will walk with you".

"If one part of the body suffers, all the other parts suffer with it. Or if one part of our body is honored [glorified], all the other parts share its honor [rejoice with it]" (1 Corinthians 12:26 EXB). Right at the very beginning, YHVH made a covenant with Adam and Eve and told them,*"Be fruitful and multiply. Populate the earth. I make you trustees of My estate, so care for My creation and rule over the fish of the sea, the birds of the sky, and every creature that roams across the earth"* (Genesis 1:28 Voice). Right there YHVH made a binding covenant between Himself and man.

A covenant needs to be sealed with something; the Bible says, *"[He has also appropriated and acknowledged us as His by] putting His seal upon us and giving us His [Holy] Spirit in our hearts as the security deposit and guarantee [of the fulfillment of His promise]"* (2 Corinthians 1:22 AMP). That seal is the power of attorney for you to call on the help of YHVH any time you need it. The power of attorney says, 'With all that I have in the power of my ring I have set a seal of life that is going to be displayed around your life and is available for you to call upon.'

The Covenant of Promise

"Then God led Abram outside and said, "Look at the sky [heavens]. There are so many stars you cannot count them. Your descendants [seed] also will be too many to count." Abram believed [put his trust/faith in] the LORD. And the LORD accepted Abram's faith, and that faith made him right with God... Abram fell into a deep sleep. While he was asleep, a very terrible [or frightening] darkness came. Then the LORD said to Abram... you, Abram, will die [go to your fathers/ancestors] in peace and will be buried at an old age. After your great-great-grandchildren are born [After the fourth generation], your people [they] will come to this land [here] again... After the sun went down, it was very dark. Suddenly a smoking fire-pot and a blazing torch [fire and smoke often represent God] passed between the halves of the dead animals [pieces; a self-curse ritual; by passing between the pieces of the sacrifice, one vowed to keep an agreement or suffer the same fate as the animals]. So on that day the LORD made an agreement [cut a covenant/treaty] with Abram and said, "I will give to your descendants [seed] the land between the river of Egypt and the great river Euphrates" (Genesis 15:5-6, 12-13, 15-18 EXB).

There was a binding agreement between YHVH and Abraham. When YHVH made the covenant with Abraham there was a power that was released in the realm of the spirit that enabled him and those with him to have victory because YHVH was with them.

Stars speak of heavenly rulership. There were two seeds that were promised to Abraham. One was the earthly seed, *"Blessing I will bless you, and multiplying I will multiply your descendants as the stars of the heaven and as the sand which is on the seashore"* (Genesis 22:17). The second one is the covenant where YHVH began to show Abraham the promise of the positional power that Israel was going to come into, YHVH said to him *"...Count the stars if you are able to number them...So shall your descendants be"* (Genesis 15:5). The first promise is for positional power, to rule over the earth, to get back what Satan took from Adam. This covenant speaks of the heavenly seed and mandates us to dispossess any usurper that may have a hold over the area of the stewardship that Adam lost but YHVH has given us through Jesus Christ. YHVH has given us power in this covenant to assert our dominion in that area and kick the usurper out; power to assert dominion and operate in the realm of the Kingdom to take away the dominion the demonic world that has held us bound. The spirit world is real even though many of us try to ignore it by putting our head in the sand, which gives our backside the opportunity to be kicked by the devil. You cannot ignore the spirit world, so YHVH has given us the ability to deal to it.

The second promise says, *"I will give to your descendants [seed] the land..."* (Genesis 15:18 EXB). YHVH was talking about a very natural seed and a very natural land, but there is a very spiritual application to this promise:

"On the same day the LORD made a covenant (promise, pledge) with Abram, saying,
"To your descendants I have given this land, from the river of Egypt to the great river Euphrates – [the land of] the Kenites and the Kenizzites and the Kadmonites and the Hittites and the Perizzites and the Rephaim, the Amorites and the Canaanites and the Girgashites and the Jebusites" (Genesis 15:18-21 AMP).

An interesting thing about this is that one of those groups of people was not a nation – that is the Rephaim, which were a race of giants. The Rephaim existed in Israel's day but Israel gained the victory over them all.

They were not a nation that possessed a place, land or position. Wherever they went they were known as the lords of the earth. In that covenant YHVH gave Abraham dominion over the highest spiritual principality that exerted pressure on the earth in his day, giving Abraham the authority and the mandate to go in there and kick the Rephaim out.

YHVH has given that to us today to go in there and kick them out. I do not know how many times I had read this verse until the Lord said, "Look and see." So I began to do a study on the giants of the earth, which was a very interesting journey.

I can remember beginning to look into some information about these giants and how they were present in Noah's day. A femur bone was discovered and documented in some records as being six feet long. (A femur is the thigh bone in the leg). That means somebody was approximately twenty-five feet high. No wonder the Israelites said, *"There we saw the giants (the descendants of Anak came from the giants); and we were like grasshoppers in our own sight, and so we were in their sight"* (Numbers 13:33). Those beings had already come out of the demonic realm, as the Bible says *"There were giants on the earth in those days, and also afterward, when the sons of God came in to the daughters of men and they bore children to them. Those were the mighty men who were of old, men of renown"* (Genesis 6:4). I wonder what happened to their spirits when they died.

The ecclesia needs to understand that YHVH is going to bring us to a place where we will have positional dominion, not just over a city, but over the tectonic plates of the earth; and that it is our job to exert the authority that YHVH has given us in the heavenly places, which is the realm of dominion where authority is exercised from.

About three or four years ago now, in my preparation time to go to a particular nation, I pressed into the realm of the spirit to see what was going on because I wanted to see the things that I would be contending with. I have dominion and I want to know that when I go somewhere, I am going to be cloaked with the armour of YHVH, stand in my role and spiritual influences are going to bow the knee because YHVH made a covenant that has given me the right to exert authority.

Some people say that we cannot do that because a corporate anointing is needed, but it is the individual believer's anointing that enables us to bring the corporate anointing to release the earth from wrong power and control.

I can remember pushing in one day and coming up against a veil in the realm of the spirit that I had never seen before and I did not understand. When I do not understand something I persistently push in until it breaks, as I want to know what is behind it, because YHVH has given me access as a son to the realm of the Kingdom. As I pushed into this veil it tore open and there was a demonic creature behind it. This creature was the most magnificent thing I had ever seen. People talk about territorial spirits, but those would be way down the food chain. I can remember looking at this thing and seeing the throne that it sat on, the realm of dominion that it had over an area of this planet, and the dominion that it had over a particular nation. I remember looking at it and thinking, "Lord, is this what you are going to bring us into?" I went, "Haaaaaaaah", and it heard me. As it turned around I saw such hatred in its eyes, but behind its eyes I also saw fear because it had been seen for the first time.

When YHVH begins to show you something in the spirit realm, you come into the inheritance of the covenant of promise because YHVH has given us the heavenly places to rule within.

The covenant of promise mandates us for war, by empowering us to execute judgment to dispossess and kick out the enemy. YHVH gave His people, Israel, the land; but they had to possess it, and dispossess who and what was there. This covenant brought Old Testament Israel and brings us today into all that Abraham had. It brings us under this blessing. Thus the anointing that flowed from Abraham can come upon us as well. It mandates us to exercise dominion over all that YHVH has given us.

The covenant of promise enables us to do the work that Abraham did. It released Israel to go and dispossess *all* that was in that land. There is coming a Caleb generation. People have spoken about the Joshua generation and the Joshua generation is doing a good job, but I am waiting, because I am a Caleb, I want the giants. Caleb went to Joshua in that day and said to him, *"And now, look, the LORD has let me live, just as He said, these forty-five years … I am eighty-five years old today. I am still as strong today … for war and for going out and coming in. So now, give me this hill country about which the LORD spoke that day, for you heard on that day that the [giant-like] Anakim were there, with great fortified cities; perhaps the LORD will be with me, and I shall drive them out just as the LORD said!"* (Joshua 14:10-12 AMP). And Caleb took the high places.

The Bible says that we will do the works that Abraham did. The Word of YHVH quickened in us builds life and produces faith and Jesus is the quickening spirit.

Faith

1) Faith is something that is imputed into us, *"The story of how faith was credited to Abraham was not recorded for him and him alone, but was written for all of us who would one day be credited for having faith in God, the One who raised Jesus our Lord from the realm of the dead. He was delivered over to death for our trespasses and raised so that we might be made right with God"* (Romans 4:23-24 VOICE).

2) Faith produces righteousness, *"He did not waver at the promise of God through unbelief, but was strengthened in faith, giving glory to God, and being fully convinced that what He had promised He was also able to perform. And therefore "it was accounted to him for righteousness"* (Romans 4:20-22). The Word says that YHVH imputes righteousness by faith. YHVH shows up and breathes into your spirit life. That is why the Word says, *"...The life which I now live in the flesh I live by faith in the Son of God, who loved me and gave Himself for me. I do not set aside the grace of God; for if righteousness comes through the law, then Christ died in vain"* (Galatians 2:20-21). It is not your faith but it is His faith in what He has given you, operating *in* you that enables you to live the life of a Christian. It is not in your own strength and you have got to build faith as well.

3) Faith produces obedience. Abraham's obedience enables us to come underneath the covering of the blessing. Because of Jesus' obedience at the cross we are able to come into His obedience and experience the provision of obedience within us.

4) Faith produces provision. The covenant brings us into the blessing of being able to see the provision of YHVH a long time before we receive it, so we are able to understand and receive that provision out of the realm of the Kingdom to possess the promise of YHVH.

The devil hates me talking on this subject. Glory! It is our excessively great pleasure and privilege to stand on the face of the devil, but you can only do it through a relationship with Jesus Christ. If you try to connect with any other spirit world or spirit realm outside of Jesus Christ, you are connecting with a demonic world. Access to YHVH is by Jesus; there is no other gateway but Jesus. It is all about Him and the price He paid. This is the only faith in the world where YHVH came looking for man. All the others are man's effort trying to find salvation.

5) Faith brings protection. The Word says this. *"I will bless those who bless you, and I will place a curse on those who harm [or curse] you. And all the people [families; clans] on earth will be blessed through you [the promises of the Abrahamic covenant]"* (Genesis 12:3 EXB). That covenant brings us into the realm of anointing that stops the demonic world laying its claw upon our life.

Because I am under a covenant, the covenant and the power that is in it *is* my protection. As I am protected by that covenant, there is provision there to invoke and release anointing and the power of YHVH on my behalf, and so I hold that covenant up in the spirit world, praying:

"Father, according to this covenant that I have walked through, according to the grafted seed of Abraham that exists in my life, the covenant that says 'those who curse you, I will curse' Father, I stand on that today."

When we hold that covenant up in the spirit world we know that, *"…The curse without cause does not come and alight [on the undeserving]"* (Proverbs 26:2 AMP). So anything which is a curse that has no legal right to alight goes back to where it has come from, because without a cause a curse cannot stay.

A Curse Defeated

Some time ago I walked through a situation where a witches circle painted a curse in occult symbols in animal blood all over the front of a church wall. I know these symbols and what they are used for and I know what the curse was. They had left a sacrificial knife with blood all over it and the animal's dismembered parts were laid in front of the church. Most Christians would wash it away, pretend it had not happened and not tell anyone. I said, "Glory to the Lord!" because we win. You see, if you get intimidated by the demonic world, it will put you out of position and then it has got possession of your power. So I went with the pastor to see what YHVH would do.

When we got there, we washed the blood off the wall and took the objects away. We burned the sacrificial knife, hammered and bent it before throwing it in the rubbish bin because I love doing things that destroy demonic power. We also burned the pieces of the animal. Then we prayed:

"Father, let this come up as a fragrance, that Your glory would come onto it and You would smite the enemy with the very curse they've laid on us," because the covenant says 'those that curse you, I will curse.' I felt led to tell the pastor that it would take three days, and then we would see YHVH begin to move.

In those three days we took our stand and held the covenant up praying:

"Father we stand under that covenant and we decree that any curse without a cause cannot alight, we stand under the provision and protection of the power of that covenant. Lord, let it be according to Your Word."

On the third day, one of the people who was an open gate prophetically in the church, suddenly had a revelation as the Lord showed her, in the realm of the spirit, what had happened that night: A huge warring angel had come into the witches circle and had started picking the people up and throwing them around the room until there was so much fear in that room that they all ran out. This prophetic sister saw this happen in her vision and shared it with us.

Right then I knew that YHVH was starting to move. Ten minutes later we got a phone call saying, "Hi, please can you help me, I was one of the people that laid a curse upon your church. Last night something happened to us and I am so afraid, please, what do I need to do? I want to ask your forgiveness, what do I need to do?" She said, "We will not go back because we are so afraid and the coven has broken up. Please help me. What do I do?" So I was able to lead her through the sinner's prayer and she got saved.

A curse that is invoked in the wrong way cannot alight; it goes back to where it has come from. That is why I am not afraid of the spirit world, because I know the provision of the covenant of YHVH through Jesus Christ for my life. YHVH has given it to us. If you can be intimidated by a demon they are going to put you out of position, and position is everything.

The keys that are given through this covenant cannot be earned. We must receive them by faith. So how do we come into the covenant promise? What do we do?

The Bible says, *"Whatever things you ask for in prayer [in accordance with God's will], believe [with confident trust] that you have received them, and they will be given to you"* (Mark 11:24 AMP). Remember you cannot connect with YHVH except through Jesus and so if you try to pray and you connect with a spirit world that is outside of the presence of YHVH you will be connecting with the demonic world. We must take ownership of our needs and ask for them to be met according to the Word of YHVH.

Spirit, Soul and Body

The Bible says, *"The LORD [He] said to Abram, "Bring me a three-year-old cow, a three-year-old goat, a three-year-old male sheep [ram], a dove [turtledove], and a young pigeon"* (Genesis 15:9 EXB).

It says these animals for sacrifice were three years old and three speaks of resurrection. A heifer speaks of the body, a she goat speaks of the soul, the ram speaks of the spirit, a turtle dove speaks of the power of the spirit of YHVH and a pigeon speaks of the power of our spirit life. These things were a covenant that Abraham made.

"Abram brought them all to God. Then Abram killed the animals and cut each of them into two pieces [split them down the middle], laying each half opposite the other half. But he did not cut the birds in half. Later large birds [or birds of prey] flew down to eat the animals [carcasses], but Abram chased them away [perhaps representing later enemies of Israel]. As the sun was going down [setting], Abram fell into a deep sleep. While he was asleep, a very terrible [or frightening] darkness came... After the sun went down, it was very dark. Suddenly a smoking firepot and a blazing torch [fire and smoke often represent God] passed between the halves of the dead animals [pieces; a self-curse ritual; by passing between the pieces of the sacrifice, one vowed to keep an agreement or suffer the same fate as the animals]. So on that day the LORD made an agreement [cut a covenant/treaty; with Abram" (Genesis 15:10-12, 17-18 EXB).

In Abraham's day when someone made a covenant it required two people to pass between the covenant. Abraham did not walk through that covenant. Abraham was asleep but saw YHVH pass through the sacrifices. YHVH is waiting for us through the seed upon us, to walk with Him through our own body, soul and spirit, to come into the position of the covenant.

The Bible says, "A *smoking firepot and a blazing torch passed between the halves of the sacrifice*". The smoking lamp is described as the incense that the priests used. Usually they had a lamp that they used to throw in the Holy of Holies and smoke would come out of it forming a cloud that the presence of YHVH could come into. The burning lamp speaks of your prayers, it speaks of the way you pray and what you build for the presence of YHVH to come into. The furnace speaks of the glory of YHVH and so your prayer and the glory of YHVH are the things that you are going to need to walk with through your covenant, which is your body, your soul and your spirit.

In the New Testament the Bible says, *"Therefore I urge you, brothers and sisters, by the mercies of God, to present your bodies [dedicating all of yourselves, set apart] as a living sacrifice, holy and well-pleasing to God"* (Romans 12:1 AMP).

Only when a sacrifice was acceptable did the two parties walk through it. Now it is interesting that, *"Large birds [or birds of prey] flew down to eat the animals [carcasses], but Abram chased them away"* (Genesis 15:11 EXB). The sense of the words, "to drive them away" means with force and persistence until you possess the promise of the provision that is in your land. Pursuing YHVH is what it is all about.

When you begin to lay your body, soul and spirit out for the presence of YHVH to invade and walk through, expect there to be a war. It happened with Abraham, it is going to happen with you. The battle goes something like this: It was difficult... it was impossible... then it was done. Possession of the covenant goes from dreaming to faith, then to assurance, then to encounter and then into position to receive.

The Bible says, *"So if you are presenting your offering at the altar, and while there you remember that your brother has something [such as a grievance or legitimate complaint] against you, leave your offering there at the altar and go. First make peace with your brother, and then come and present your offering"* (Matthew 5:23-24 AMP). One of the hindrances facing the ecclesia coming into possession of the promise in these covenants is the attitude we have towards our brother and sister.

Your family has a body life, a soul life and a spirit life; your church has a body life, a soul life and a spirit life; your city has a body life, a soul life and a spirit life; your nation has a body life, a soul life and a spirit life. YHVH wants to walk through them all, but it starts first with you possessing the promise of the covenant. *"…First here in Jerusalem, then beyond to Judea and Samaria, and finally to the farthest places on earth"* (Acts 1:8 VOICE).

It is all about position, positioning ourselves for our promise and coming into the provision of the power related to it. There are some aspects of importance in the process of possession of this covenant. It takes work. In those days all they had were knives and it would take approximately two or three hours to divide an animal.

Our problem is that many of us have never walked through these covenants with YHVH. Unless you walk through them do not expect to have the provision of the power that is behind them. YHVH wants us to possess these covenants and hold them inside our hearts because they are places of exchange. All that is mine is His and all that He has becomes mine. As you can see – it is a really greedy covenant. So all that I have remains mine, but all of His is mine now too. But then all that I have becomes His, and all that is His remains His anyway. I am greedy when it comes to the power of the provision of these covenants, because I want it all. I do not just want a little piece.

You have got to get hold of the Word of YHVH, embrace it, lay hold of it and engage it until it begins to work for your life. When you engage something it is not a shallow or timid action. Engaging something is an aggressive action. The Bible says, *"From the days of John the Baptist until now the kingdom of heaven suffers violent assault, and violent men seize it by force [as a precious prize]"* (Matthew 11:12 AMP). You have got to be forceful when you lay hold of the Word of YHVH and forceful with the spirit world, until you possess the promise that is in it. Laying hold of the Word of YHVH is not a nice meek, timid thing. We need to speak it into being: "Father, I thank you that I walk in that", with a totally different attitude behind it that *"calls things that did not exist into existence"* (Romans 4:17 EXB). YHVH wants us to lay hold of what He has for us in His promises.

One of the ways of possessing the covenant is prayer. Prayer is the working part of coming into possession and dividing your body, soul and spirit, so that the power of YHVH can work through it. With this reading the Word and holding the Word in the spirit world; meditating upon the Word until the revelation of what is in it becomes yours; holding it and building a picture until you can invade the realm of the Kingdom and step into that realm. You have got to guard it by strongly praying in the Holy Spirit, building your spirit man until there is a vibrant process of life coming out of your spirit. People say to me, "How do you get so much energy?" Well, I just lock into Holy Spirit where my power comes from and put my finger in the spiritual power socket.

The year I began to work on this covenant in my life I got hit by lightning and I lived to tell the tale. I had already been wondering about how to go into the spirit and YHVH just opened the door. So for a fraction of a second when the blue light hit the building, I was standing on the roof in pouring rain, totally wet, holding a ladder that went down to the ground. This lightning went BOOM and did sixty-five thousand dollars worth of damage to all the electrics in my building, the lightning went BOOM and I went CRACK as I found a gateway!

You spend time praying in tongues and begin to remember what happened and push in the moment the door opens. Once you have been there, you can go there again. When you go there again the access route gets faster for the next time.

The Covenant of the blood of Jesus

YHVH has a lot of names including Jehovah Jireh, our provider and Jehovah Nissi, our victory in battle, promising the full supply of everything that is in His Name, all that He carries, every bit of power, dominion, might, authority and provision in the Name. We carry that covenant because of the blood of Jesus; it is sealed upon our lives through YHVH's desire to bring us back into His Name, because He wants a family that bears His Name.

"You must know (recognize) that you were redeemed (ransomed) from the useless (fruitless) way of living inherited by tradition from [your] forefathers, not with corruptible things [such as] silver and gold, but [you were purchased]

with the precious blood of Christ (the Messiah), like that of a [sacrificial] lamb without blemish or spot.

It is true that He was chosen and foreordained (destined and foreknown for it) before the foundation of the world, but He was brought out to public view (made manifest) in these last days (at the end of the times) for the sake of you.

Through Him you believe in (adhere to, rely on) God, Who raised Him up from the dead and gave Him honor and glory, so that your faith and hope are [centered and rest] in God." (1 Peter 1:18-21 AMP).

Without the shedding of Jesus' blood there would have been no rising from the dead. Rising from the dead is not about just having a relationship with YHVH; it is raising you out of the death of the record of the DNA of your life, raising you into something different; that is resurrection. I am looking forward to having a body like Jesus had on the mountain. (Matthew 17:1-2).

Life in the blood of Jesus

"For the life of the flesh is in the blood, and I have given it to you upon the altar to make atonement for your souls; for it is the blood that makes atonement for the soul.' Therefore I said to the children of Israel, 'No one among you shall eat blood, nor shall any stranger who dwells among you eat blood'" (Leviticus 17:11-12).

This says that the life of the flesh is in the blood; in the blood dwells the soul of YHVH's Son. Jesus said, *"I am the way, the truth, and the life"* (John 14:6). To have life you have got to have an expression in life; an expression is dictated by what your soul symbolises; who you are is dictated by your soul, not by your body. It is read by your body, but your soul has feelings, it has emotions, choice, will, mind and imagination woven inside it; that begins to display who you are. Jesus' blood carries the soul of Christ's life in it, wanting you to display that life to the world around you.

Because of Jesus' obedience to the Father's Will, He sanctifies our disobedience, uniting our will with His. Because of His obedience to the Father's will, I am able to embrace His will, in the place of mine. In that blood covenant when Jesus gave His life, with that life Jesus surrendered His will so that my disobedience can embrace His will and say, 'Father, I am willing. I am willing to die for You, Jesus.' It is not my will then, it is Jesus' will. *"...The life which I now live in the flesh I live by faith in the Son of God, who loved me and gave Himself for me"* (Galatians 2:20). It is not our faith, it is by the faith of the Son of YHVH who gave Himself for you and me. That is how we live, by His faith, because we cannot do anything of ourselves. YHVH does everything for us and says, "Here is My part, all I want is surrender".

When we yolk ourselves to that covenant, the resurrection power that is in it becomes ours. There is resurrection life in that covenant that will raise us up in the dead places of our lives. I have learned that a right demanded from someone is a never ending grave. It is a grave without ends on it, and many of us are caught in 'rights of life'.

Cleansing Power

"Now may the God of peace who brought up our Lord Jesus from the dead, that great Shepherd of the sheep, through the blood of the everlasting covenant make you complete in every good work to do His will..." Hebrews 13:20-21.

The blood opens the graves; where Jesus Christ's blood is there is resurrection power. The blood of Jesus deals with the power of sin in our lives by changing it from one thing, cleansing it and making it into something different. This is a really disgusting fact but it is true: when you work on motors as a mechanic your hands get really greasy. If you were to take a bucket of blood and wash your hands in that blood, every single bit of dirt and oil would come off your hands. This is a natural fact, you would have taken filthy-dirty, greasy hands that need cleaning and scouring agents to get the grease off them, and washing in that blood would remove the stain on you completely. If that is in the natural, how much more true is it in the spiritual. When we wash ourselves in the blood, this removes the stain of the record of sin that is in our lives; and how much more power is in us to apply to our lives by faith when we have communion?

When you take communion you are taking the washing power of the blood of Jesus into your body, to clean you from the inside out, because it is from the inside that you and I change, not from the outside. That is why we eat it and drink it, because YHVH wants to conform us on the inside; the same power that raised Christ from the dead is now working in you to conform you into the image of the Son of YHVH. *"He who raised Christ from the dead will also give life to your mortal bodies through His Spirit…Who will transform our lowly body that it may be conformed to His glorious body…"* (Romans 8:11, Philippians 3:21).

The blood redeems us by resurrection power, reconciles us and joins us together again with the presence of YHVH, bringing unity, *"Being justified freely by His grace through the redemption that is in Christ Jesus, whom God set forth as a propitiation by His blood, through faith, to demonstrate His righteousness, because in His forbearance God had passed over the sins that were previously committed"* (Romans 3:24-25).

"But if we walk in the light as He is in the light, we have fellowship with one another, and the blood of Jesus Christ His Son cleanses us from all sin" (1 John 1:7). The Bible says here that the blood of Jesus cleanses us from all of our sin; is there anything left outside of all? When the Bible says 'all' it means all. So you can look at the worst thing you have done and say 'all', you can look at the foulest thing you have done in the deepest darkest secret of your heart and you can say to it 'all'. All my sin! When the Word says it cleanses you it means it has gone, without record. It cannot be seen and it cannot be called upon.

Often when the enemy gets into our minds, hearts and lives it is to accuse us. The only reason he can accuse you is because you have not put your **all** under the blood of Jesus. Everything is done in the realm of the spirit. When you make the blood of Jesus your all, the enemy has no grounds for accusation against your life. The accuser goes into the court room and Jesus says, "All. Speak to the hand!" You present yourself in the realm of the spirit and start to do warfare, the demons shout, 'Aarrr!' and you say, 'All. Speak to the hand!' Why? Because Father's hand is in your hand.

The blood of Jesus sets us into service, *"How much more shall the blood of Christ, who through the eternal Spirit offered Himself without spot to God, cleanse your conscience from dead works to serve the living God?"* (Heb 9:14). A dead work is doing your own thing; wherever you have done your own thing the blood of Christ is available to set you to serve the Living God. You can go from serving yourself to serving

YHVH. But you have got to apply it to your life; it takes effort to do that, it is called the cross.

The blood of Jesus cleanses our conscience from dead works. The conscience is a vital ingredient in your soul, it is one of the gateways of the soul (see Ian's manual, Gateways of the Three-Fold Nature of Man). The conscience can be seared; the blood of Jesus heals your conscience and brings a God consciousness into your life; an awareness of the presence of YHVH. Some people ask me if I am always aware of the presence of YHVH. Yes I am. As He moves I want to follow; it is not because I am so good, it is because my conscience has been cleansed and I want to stay near purity. I want to find the fountain of the purity of Heaven and that is in the presence of YHVH.

"Therefore, brethren, having boldness to enter the Holiest by the blood of Jesus, by a new and living way which He consecrated for us, through the veil, that is, His flesh, and having a High Priest over the house of God, let us draw near with a true heart in full assurance of faith, having our hearts sprinkled from an evil conscience and our bodies washed with pure water" (Hebrews 10:19-22).

You cannot come into the glory of the presence of YHVH and enter into the Holy Place of YHVH unless you have applied the blood of Jesus to your life.

The priests knew very well what would happen. They used to go in just once a year, but the Bible says we can come boldly before Him any time, *"Therefore, brothers and sisters, we have boldness to enter into the Holies by the blood of Yeshua. He inaugurated a new and living way for us through the curtain – that is, His flesh"* (Hebrews 10:19-20 TLV).

We can come boldly into His presence, we can trespass in there because of the blood; because it has given us power to go there; it has given us authority and mandated us to go there. The priest used to have sacrifices to do over a long period of days; they used to take animal blood and sprinkle it over everything to go through this religious process of cleansing. The priest knew if the blood was not acceptable he would become a crisp! They used to wear these little tinkly bells on the base of their robes so that when they moved around, the poor guys on the outside knew that they were still alive. They used to tie a rope to the High Priest's ankle because if that blood was not acceptable, he would die inside there and these guys were not allowed to go in there, even if the High Priest was dead! They would pull him out by the rope. They knew about the blood, they knew about its cleansing power and what it would do to set us in the place, to enable us to come before the glory.

"Then Jesus said to them, "Most assuredly, I say to you, unless you eat the flesh of the Son of Man and drink His blood, you have no life in you. Whoever eats My flesh and drinks My blood has eternal life, and I will raise him up at the last day. For My flesh is food indeed, and My blood is drink indeed. He who eats My flesh and drinks My blood abides in Me, and I in him " (John 6:53-56).

The blood of Jesus leads us into resurrection life. When we take communion we are partakers of the very essence of YHVH which releases resurrection life in us.

"And they overcame him by the blood of the Lamb and by the word of their testimony, and they did not love their lives to the death" (Revelation 12:11).

When we have the blood we can go anywhere, even right into the very pit of Hell. You can go anywhere because the blood gives you access. The reason many people have struggled in spiritual warfare is because of their lack of knowledge of the blood of Jesus and what it gives you access to. Devils scream when you turn up and you are covered in the blood of Christ because they see their end. They are tormented by the power of the blood because they see their judgement. You symbolise all that they wanted but could never have and they hate you for it. But they cannot touch you because when you are under that blood the evil one touches you not. (1 John 5:18).

The blood of Jesus produces the nature of the Kingdom in us and around us; it makes us vessels equipped for war; it makes us purified for position as heirs; it makes us vessels mandated for dominion; it makes us vessels clothed with righteousness; it makes us vessels prepared for power. So what does it mean for you and me today?

For you and I to live under the covenant of the blood of Jesus means that we have dominion, we have power, we have position; we have righteousness, we have preparation; we have all that we need in His name over our lives. The name and the blood of

Jesus becomes a banner that tells the enemy, 'Don't come near me!'

Doing the Stuff

So how do we do this? We do it by taking communion in faith. You have got to exercise it by faith because it pleases the Father to see you do something in faith – believing that it is going to happen; believing that there is a reality you are stepping into when you take it. When I apply it to my life I step into the reality of all the provision that YHVH has for me. I get excited about this because it means that when I am covered in the blood of Jesus I represent the worst nightmare to the enemy. The nightmare that says, "Jehovah Nissi, Jehovah Rapha, Jehovah Tsidkenu, Jehovah Jireh…" The enemy does not see you, he sees God! Because the covenant brings you into the provision of all that is God's.

We enter into this by prayer; prayer is not just saying words. The Bible says, "…*The kingdom of heaven suffers violence, and the violent take it by force*" (Matthew 11:12). The forceful ones enforce it and bring it down. So when you pray about the blood of Jesus it is, "Father, thank You for the blood! The blood applies to my life and changes me into a son that has dominion!" YHVH wants to change us and make us into who we should have been per our faith confession; yoking ourselves to something that is not necessarily seen with the eye. "Father I yoke myself to the blood of Jesus, I yoke myself to it today in Jesus Name!" Instead of praying with resignation, "Oh Lord I carry the yoke of the blood and my spouse is my cross…!" It is about your personal walk with YHVH, not about your relationship with somebody else.

We meditate, which is not sitting there with your legs crossed going, "Umm…!" It is not sitting there focusing on a rock and thinking you are going to get life out of it, because you will connect with the realm that is in darkness! Meditating means having your mind, heart, thoughts and desires so captivated with the object of your desire that you believe you have it. When I am praying about being yoked to the blood of Jesus over my life, I see this great big thing come down over my life; and that leads me into the Kingdom of Heaven because wherever the blood of Jesus is I am yoked to the Kingdom of Heaven. I am yoked to the glory, to the provision of the names of God, to His power and to the anointing.

Engage the Kingdom

Take something about this teaching that has really spoken to you and for five minutes, pray in tongues with your mind focused on that point or aspect, drawing and yoking yourself to displaying it. You need to have your mind engaged so that you are not just praying in tongues robotically. It means focusing into where the Kingdom of God is within you; engaging that Kingdom inside you and extending that Kingdom to begin to believe to be yoked to the portion of what you are seeing. Whatever you see, you can have, "...*According to your faith, let it be done for you*" (Matthew 9:29 TLV). This is a major principle: whatever the eye hooks into multiplies; whatever you see will multiply in your life so you can have it.

"Father I want to get hold of this thing! This reality is going to be mine!" Hold onto it and pull on it.

The Bible says, "...*the kingdom of God is within you*" (Luke 17:21). It is this Kingdom I am looking to manifest on the outside of me. I am not looking for something to come out of Heaven to me to touch my life. I am looking to take what is in me, to release it around my life, to change my life. So I am engaging the Kingdom of God that is within me; that is where my spirit is, where the flow of the glory is coming from the inside of me to the outside of me. Carry on praying with that knowledge.

The Word says that we overcome by the blood of the Lamb (Revelation 12:11). Take a secret area of your life that you have wrestled with, present it before the Lord and declare the blood of Jesus over that thing in your life. This is about your personal life, not about Jane or John down the road, this is about you. With the focus inside your mind and heart, "God it is the blood of Jesus that gives me the victory; it is Your blood, I overcome this by the blood of the Lamb; I declare the blood of Jesus over this; this thing is redeemed from that power by the blood of Jesus, it is under the blood, hallelujah!" And simultaneously pray in tongues. You can go in and out of this and you do not have to get all spiritual to do it.

There is another aspect to the blood. In the provision in Christ my feet are like fine brass; I have shoes of brass on; which means when I stand on his head, he is not going to bruise my heel because my feet are like fine brass to the enemy. Which means I can do whatever I like with him; in fact, I am going to enjoy standing all over him because he has tormented my life enough! Now it is our turn to stamp all over him.

In Genesis, YHVH said to the devil, *"What you have done carries great consequences. Now you are cursed ... You will writhe on your belly forever, consuming the dust out of which man was made. I will make you and your brood enemies of the woman and all her children; The woman's child will stomp your head, and you will strike his heel"* (Genesis 3:14-15 Voice).

In Revelation it says, *"I saw ... One like the Son of Man ... His head and hair were white like wool, as white as snow, and His eyes like a flame of fire; His feet were like fine brass, as if refined in a furnace..."* (Revelation 1:12-15).

The issue you prayed under the blood, see that thing under your feet; you are standing on the top of it with victory in your mouth and in your heart; with the desire of YHVH to see that thing defeated in your life as you pray in tongues. Hallelujah!

I guarantee you, if you do this every day for 21 days, your life will begin to change; because you are applying what the Word says it is potentially possible for us in our personal lives today.

Activation

I am going to get you to do one thing, and that is to begin to yoke yourself to the presence of the Holy Ghost, and what I do when I yoke myself to the presence of God is, in my mind's eye I see a yoke coming over me, like this. Then it encompasses around my body and around my life and then what I do is I step next to the Holy Spirit like this and I latch on to His yoke. I latch on to His yoke and His presence.

So what I am going to get you to do is to pray in tongues and I want you to seat yourself in the place where your spirit man is, spend five minutes doing that and then we are going to begin to turn to the Holy Spirit. While you are praying in tongues, in your mind, I want you to begin to ask Him, "Lord, I want to be yoked to You. Holy Spirit, I want to be yoked to You because You lead me to Jesus, and Jesus I want to be yoked to You because You are going to lead me to the Father."

I am going to get you to begin to pray, and I am going to begin to get you to put over your life the yoke of the Holy Spirit. "Lord I yoke myself to Your presence, Lord, I want to be led by You into all truth, I yoke myself to Your presence." You have got to set your heart and begin to desire, begin to allow the desire to rise up inside you. "Lord, I want to be yoked to You, Holy Spirit I want to be yoked."

"Lord I want to be yoked to Your glory, Holy Spirit I want to be yoked to You. Lord I want to be yoked to You. Lord I desire to be yoked to You as my Rabbi. Holy Spirit I desire to be yoked to You as my Rabbi. Lord I turn to You today. Lord I take Your yoke, I take Your yoke over my life today and I join myself with Your desire for me. I join myself with Your presence today. Lord I yoke myself to You. Holy Spirit I yoke myself to Your desire for my life. I yoke myself to Your destiny for my life. I yoke myself to the truth about my life. I yoke myself to Your purpose for my life. Lord, I yoke myself to You today. Holy Spirit thank You. Thank You that You are my leader and my guide, and You will lead me into all truth. Holy Spirit thank You. Thank You Holy Spirit that I can hear Your voice, that I can feel Your glory and Your prompting. Lord, I choose to respond to Your voice today. Lord You are the only one, You are the only one that I choose to give the right to guide me. Holy Spirit thank You. Holy Spirit thank You, that I am going to hear You, that I am going to be close to You and You will be close to me, because all that You have is now at my disposal, and Lord all that I have I give to You and make at Your disposal. Thank You Holy Spirit. Thank You Lord."

You can go through and do this with Jesus and do it with the Father.

Chapter 3
Familiar Spirits

The word "familiar" means: to be deeply acquainted with, to be well known, to be intimate or excessively informal. The Hebrew word that is used in the Bible to describe a familiar spirit is pronounced "obe". It is spelt ob and translated into English it means a leather bottle[2].

These leather bottles were very supple, so that they would be able to fit into hidden areas of a person's pack and would mould around their back without causing them harm or showing on the outside. These leather bottles were designed to be carried in the desert in really dry regions so the person had water to drink. They would conform to odd shapes and could squeeze into little hidden nooks and crannies to be hidden or carried in places that made them very difficult to find, especially if people were going into war, so that in the battlefield they had a way of storing essential water.

A leather bottle would be used to carry essential water and it would be under a protective covering that the enemy would not be able to get through to. Similarly in our lives when a demonic spirit attaches to our soul, as a familiar spirit, they come and they attach deep inside our souls with a huge covering over them that stops YHVH accessing those areas of us. Often, when we are in dry places, we drink from other fountains that are outside of the presence of God and the place where we can connect with the glory of God in our spirit.

---

[2] Strong's Concordance "בוֹא" in Hebrew (178) transliterated as ob, pronounced obe, which occurs 17 times in the Bible to mean bottle made of animal skin, or familiar spirit/medium or one who mutters.

Just to give you some background, a familiar spirit is a particular type of spirit so named because of its chief characteristic, familiarity with a person, their sin and their behaviour. Often in a relationship, the sharing of intimate areas through communication with one another forms a bond that grows between two people. A familiar spirit bonds itself in the same way to us by becoming familiar. This demonic spirit bonds itself to the very nature of the soul of a person, through life's struggles, through repetitive sin and hidden thought patterns, getting into the intimate hidden areas of our lives. They will always remain in the dark but be very personally involved in the life of a person. Because a familiar spirit's chief characteristic is the medium of communication, such familiar spirits often speak to us through our thought life and imagination. Often times they come as the little whispers that we hear. Little whispers that go like this, "They don't really like you, do they?", "She really hates you" or "Didn't you know your mother didn't like you?"

Familiar spirits want to remain hidden inside of our lives so that they can influence us and sit in that place of our need so that we will drink from their water source and from the facility of their sin and their power. In that place, as we are drinking from them, we find that we get connected and actually become tied to them. So instead of finding the voice of YHVH and being able to release His life and His Spirit around us we release something else and it is from the attachments of familiar spirits through our lives.

"Some people say, "Ask the mediums and fortune-tellers [necromancers; spiritists], who whisper [or chirp] and mutter [using incantations to call up spirits; 1 Sam. 28:8–11], what to do." But I tell you that people should ask their God for help" (Isaiah 8:19 EXB).

Those familiar spirits provide information. They are called familiar spirits because their chief characteristic is relational connection to information about your life. We often have the familiarity and closeness of a relationship with these demon spirits that lodge inside our soul and connect to us, influencing the way we think and behave. They can often be the driving force behind repetitive sin cycles. Where there is sexual misconduct or sexual connection outside marriage, demonic familiar spirits lodge into those areas of our lives and drive us into promiscuity. Familiar spirits drive us into sexual connection and then our soul gets tied to that person. As we are driven into wrong connection with person after person our soul gets scattered and those demon spirits attach onto that scattering of our soul, preventing us from being able to form proper deep committed connections with YHVH or with the one that we were designed to marry.

Familiar spirits lodge deep inside of us and often we do not even know they are there. The only way I began to recognise them was as I began to challenge the voices that I would hear inside myself.

Discerning the Voice of Familiar Spirits

To identify the voice of a familiar spirit inside your brain:
1) Does it produce life?
2) Has it got love in it?
3) Is it YHVH centered and is it Word centered?
If the answer is no to each of these questions, then the voice has its roots in the voice of a familiar spirit.

Those familiar spirits are often attached to the areas of sin we live in. They are controllers that encourage and form the bondages or strongholds being established towards a certain sin pattern or a bent towards a certain type of sin. They are intimate activators, tempting an individual to fall into sin or to yield to a particular type of sin nature. These things get inside our spirit and lodge there, shut us down and make us afraid. Often they are the things that say, "YHVH won't accept you, you're a sinner. You fell into sin yesterday, how do you think Father feels about you doing that again and again and again, you know He doesn't love you because you do that."

Have you had thoughts like that? The issue is not that they assail your life; the issue is the way you respond to them. Eventually you can silence the voice of the stranger, and that is what they are. They are the stranger's voices in the sheepfold inside your own soul that speak to you, being affirmation outside of the presence of the glory and the power of YHVH, *"Most assuredly, I say to you, he who does not enter the sheepfold by the door, but climbs up some other way, the same is a thief and a robber. But he who enters by the door is the shepherd of the sheep. To him the doorkeeper opens, and the sheep hear his voice; and he calls his own sheep by name and leads them out. And when he brings out his own sheep, he goes before them; and the sheep follow him, for they know his voice. Yet they will by no means follow a stranger but will flee from him, for they do not know the voice of strangers... The thief does not come except to steal, and to kill, and to destroy. I have come that they may have life, and that they may have it more abundantly"* (John 10:1-5, 10).

I really want to expose these things because so many Christians hear the voice of familiar spirits and they do not know how to silence them or to shut them down in the spirit world so they can begin to actively hear the voice of YHVH speaking to them in a correct way.

Witchcraft

A familiar spirit is a demon spirit that expresses itself through and in the life of a person. They are very common where witchcraft is involved. Witchcraft does not only mean the issue of mediums or direct occult influence, but it also involves control, domination and manipulation. You may find that inside your mind, familiar spirits will come and they will speak to you saying things like, "You don't have to take that." Or, "How do you think it feels to be like that?" Or they will come into someone's mind and say, "You must have control of your family, don't you know your wife must submit to you?" The familiar spirit avoids the issue of telling the husband that he must love his wife first and lay his life down for her (Ephesians 5:25). Familiar spirits know part of the truth and use the law to bring a false control or governing influence over our lives to make us respond, which makes us fall into sin. They do not know the whole truth, they just want to keep our spirit man bound and locked up. Often familiar spirits are found around harassing circumstances. They would rob our faith, they steal our hope and destroy our beliefs in who we are supposed to be.

A person called a medium or fortune teller will have familiar spirits that use them and speak through them. The Word of God tells us that those who have familiar spirits are defiled by them. *"Give no regard to mediums and familiar spirits; do not seek after them, to be defiled by them: I am the LORD your God"* (Leviticus 19:31).

Now, sometimes people will think they see a dead loved one

appear to them, and they will say "Oh, I saw my aunty the other day". Well they did not see their aunty, it says that *"...It is destined that men die only once, and after that comes judgment"* (Hebrews 9:27 TLB). Without salvation through Jesus you live, you die and you go straight to hell. But the demonic spirits attached to your life (familiar spirits) are so familiar with your character, your personality, your responses and the intimate areas of your life where you struggle that they begin to take on your image. So the thing that you see appearing to you is a familiar demonic spirit that was attached to a person's life before they died. The familiar spirit comes visiting because it has a generational access through the gate of generational sin to connect with your life.

These things are real because we live in a spirit world, but we need to learn that the spirit realm is subject to us and there are ways to deal with them.

Leviticus 20:27 says those who have familiar spirits must be put to death. This verse speaks of us in our lives today in the areas of our brokenness, where there are familiar spirit attachments. Those areas of our lives must be put to death through the power of YHVH and connection with the cross of Christ. We must allow YHVH to work His way into those areas of our lives to cause destruction to the strongholds and the embattlements that form in our spirit. *"When a strong man armed keeps his palace, his goods are in peace: But when a stronger than he shall come upon him, and overcome him, he takes from him all his armor in which he trusted, and divides his spoils"* (Luke 11:21-22 KJ2000). The word *strongman* means one who has a fortress, or embattlement established in the life of a person, where he can hold them captive and control what goes in and out of his life.

The chief characteristic of familiar spirits is deception. This is the main way they stay and operate through and around a person's life. Usually we accept them as, "Oh, that's just my lot in life. I'm just like that." This gives them the right to lodge inside our soul because we do not want that part of our life brought into and under the hand of YHVH. This enables them to entangle and ensnare the lives of believers as well as non-believers. I have found that non-believers are more subject to the workings of familiar spirits. That is why you find in nightclubs that demon spirits attach to the soul life or the atmosphere and begin to influence people. Their goal is to cause the soul of a person to be scattered, and so they attach to the spirit and soul life. As they begin to influence people there is a sense of promiscuity and lust that becomes a drive from the need for intimacy. These types of driven-ness are really what familiar spirits want to express through a person's life.

In a Christian's life they drive us in the areas of our sin. There are sin habit patterns that we form in our lives, and in those sin habit patterns we are bowing down to demon spirits saying, "Here is my sacrifice to you today, receive it from my hand." I know this is pretty blunt, but it is the truth. Whenever you find yourself being driven like that, you need to look for the source. You will generally find it has some type of familiar spirit attachment that will remain hidden until it can express its desire through a person. When you sin, you actually allow a spirit being to express its desire through you.

Counterfeit for Holy Spirit

A familiar spirit is a direct counterfeit for Holy Spirit. Holy Spirit comforts, directs, reveals, empowers and leads us to Christ, and who we are in God, *"But the Helper (Comforter, Advocate, Intercessor – Counselor, Strengthener, Standby), the Holy Spirit, whom the Father will send in My name [in My place, to represent Me and act on My behalf], He will teach you all things..."* (John 14:26).

A familiar spirit demands *"...That they may come to their senses and escape from the trap of the devil, having been held captive by him to do his will"* (2 Timothy 2:26 AMP).

It comforts us in our sin, *"...stand up against all the schemes and the strategies and the deceits of the devil"* (Ephesians 6:11 AMP).

It hides us from the truth: *"...The god of this world [Satan] has blinded the minds of the unbelieving to prevent them from seeing the illuminating light of the gospel of the glory of Christ, who is the image of God"* (2 Corinthians 4:4 AMP).

Familiar spirits defile us and remind us of our sin nature. *"When the unclean spirit ... brings seven other spirits more evil than itself, and they go in [the person] and live there; and the last state of that person becomes worse than the first"* (Luke 11:24-26 AMP).

Familiar spirits are the accusers that bring condemnation and make us want to hide. *"...The accuser of our [believing] brothers and sisters has been thrown down [at last], he who accuses them and keeps bringing charges [of sinful behavior] against them before our God day and night"* (Revelation 12:10 AMP).

Holy Spirit convicts us and leads us to repentance and walking in the light: *"When He comes, He will convict the world about sin, righteousness, and judgment: concerning sin, because they do not believe in Me"* (John 16:8-9 TLV). In the body of Christ today you will find that people do not want to be open with their sin because there is a big finger pointing at them inside themselves. They hear it saying, "Don't tell anyone, because if you tell them, what will they think of you?" That is the voice of a familiar spirit attachment to a person's soul. The Word says, *"If we walk in the light as He Himself is in the light, we have fellowship with one another and the blood of His Son Yeshua purifies us from all sin"* (1 John 1:7 TLV).

Familiar spirits want you to remain in darkness in the areas of your vulnerability so that they can keep access to your soul to maintain you making sacrifices to them by listening to their voice. As you read this, if you find yourself hearing, "No, I don't really want to do that," examine the voice, as the Word says, *"do not believe every spirit, but test the spirits, whether they are of God"* (1 John 4:1). Does it produce life? Does it produce the character of YHVH – peace, love and joy? If it does not, where is it from?

Maybe it is a demon spirit, attached to your soul, speaking in your mind, attached to the familiar cycles of your sin that controls and drives you. Familiar spirits are often the driving force that is behind the sin nature that makes us desire to sin and to keep our sin hidden, stopping YHVH and others from walking with us through our lives because these familiar spirits want to walk with us through our life. They want us to hold their hand instead of us holding the Father's hand and allowing Him to walk in our lives.

How to Identify the Effects of Familiar Spirits

1) What do you do in secret? Your behaviour in secret is an indicator of what is residing in your spirit.

2) What is our behavior around others, particularly in regard to

gossip? People who gossip in churches often have familiar spirits attached to them because information to a familiar spirit is power.

People who are controlled by familiar spirits and gossip to one another can form a collusion together in the spirit as two demons connect, creating judgment together in agreement against another.

Those voices of familiar spirits speak in our minds and hearts, becoming so familiar with our habit patterns and the processes of our thought lives that they ensnare us, enslave us and establish an embattlement and a fortress inside our soul. We need those fortresses inside ourselves to be assailed, identified, torn down and the voices silenced in Jesus name.

3) What are the hidden thought patterns that go on inside your mind where no one sees except you and God? Thought patterns and flickering images often have attachments of familiar spirits to them. We become soul tied to the familiar spirit and feed from it instead of from the presence of God. Fantasies, pornography, and fantasy role play in our minds where we are always the fastest car driver, the highest and fastest ball thrower, the best mother, and the best in whatever situation. Those things sometimes have connections to familiar spirits because they live in our fantasies and want us to believe something that we are not. They make you live out of the spirit realm they create by feeding you false information, because it comforts your soul. This image, imagination or false fantasy makes you feel good so you commune with it and sit there drinking from it thinking, "Yeah that would be really great… imagine driving that thing. Boy wouldn't that be great, just driving that car down the road. Can you imagine sitting inside it?" You get caught in the fantasy, and it is this voice that actively works with that fantasy that draws you away from the voice of YHVH.

The little whispers that come into our thought life and imagination are the work of familiar spirits, especially when a form of sin or a suggestion to sin is involved. Demons say in our minds, "People can't see it, so it doesn't really matter, does it? It doesn't really matter if you sin, well God will forgive you, won't He?" Those voices are the voices of familiar spirits in our minds. We need to exercise dominion and take authority over them.

Often these whispers can be heard in the first person. Things like, "I really need that; I wonder what they are thinking; I wonder if they are talking about me?" Their aim is to wind you up in rejection, so it locks you up from communing and keeping an open spirit and connection towards the presence of YHVH.

When you deal with the power of a familiar spirit, it becomes easier to hear and discern the voice of Holy Spirit because your mind is not cluttered and crowded with the hidden thought patterns that produce death in us. When our minds and hearts are free from the clutter of these voices it becomes very easy to tune our spirit man into different flows of the anointing and heavenly realms of the Kingdom that YHVH exists in and expresses Himself through. It enables us to connect and commune with YHVH in a much clearer and easier way. One of the reasons many of us do not hear from YHVH is because our ears are blocked by familiar spirit attachments that do not want us to hear the words of freedom, liberty and love that YHVH brings to release to us.

Discipleship Mentoring
In the group we mentor and disciple we have training times of connection with YHVH. We take young people away for an impact weekend and one of the sessions is about how to hear the love whispers of the Father. We teach them about it and then we send them away and encourage them to begin to commune and connect with the Father. In that place they hear the Father say things like, "I love you, I want you to draw close to Me, I want you to hold Me, son / daughter. I want you to learn of Me and connect with Me. I have many things I want to tell you." The voice of the Father never stops wooing us. Our Father's voice woos us like a lover, *"Therefore, behold, I will allure her, Will bring her into the wilderness, and speak comfort to her* (Hosea 2:14). The problem is that our ears are often deafened and indifferent to hear the voice of our Father wooing us.

Dopamine
Our sin cycles often produce a chemical release inside our body called dopamine. Dopamine produces a sense of well-being, of feeling satisfied, or a pleasure reward. Where familiar spirits are attached, dopamine is released in our life when we draw

on the habit pattern of sin, which brings a sense of fulfilment. The interesting thing is that it has been chemically proven in laboratories that a person who is connected to YHVH in a deep, intimate and meaningful way also has dopamine released into their bloodstream when they begin to commune with Him. This brings a sense of belonging, acceptance, kinship and security and breaks the power that sin has on us because we find another security and another way to have our needs met. We are a spirit being with a soul in a physical body. Our body's needs can be met in a place of deep communion and connection with the presence of YHVH. We need to learn to connect with Him and pursue Him into every secret place of our life. We must allow YHVH to captivate us so that all that matters is Him. We must allow Him to treasure and captivate our hearts so that our heart is turned towards the voice of Holy Spirit. That does not come by you disciplining your flesh; it comes by you focusing and connecting with the presence of YHVH inside you. Then out of that connection comes a release of the power and the glory of YHVH to transform and transfigure your soul and bring you into a different place of communion with Him. It brings great contentment to know that YHVH has said, "Son, I love you."

Familiar spirits are the enemies of the cross and our number one personal enemy. They will always remind us of what you and I are in the normal and natural life and hinder us walking into who we are – the spirit life of YHVH.

Self-Pity

Rejection, loneliness, abandonment, isolation and the fear of the opinions of other people are some of the familiar spirits that assail our lives in waves. Self-pity is generated inside of us out of deep need, rejection and loneliness. Familiar spirits of self-pity suggest things like, "You hate yourself, don't you?" They often dwell around the need of affirmation of people, so they will affirm us by saying things like, "You're just great aren't you?" The little whispers flicker in and out of our brain, and in and out of our ear. The little spirits become so familiar with our habit patterns in areas of our lives that we struggle with, that they influence and shut us down, blocking our communing and connecting with YHVH. Very often they will come and their voices will be a lot louder when we are a lot lower in the spirit. When your spirit life is not very active, you may find that you are assailed by voices that seem to go on in your mind and you do not know why they are there. Some people say, "Well that's just my lot in life," and inside of you this thing would say, "Yeah it is. It doesn't really matter, does it?"

You may have different things that assail you. Some people have tormenting thoughts about death. That is a familiar spirit that is attached to them making them think that way. Whatever captivates your mind captivates you. If you can identify the emotional fruit the voice creates inside of you then you can identify the spirit that is connected to it. It may be a spirit of lust or a spirit of hate. When you are feeling rejection and a voice in your feelings speaks about rejection it is a spirit of rejection. When it speaks to you about loneliness and isolation, it is a spirit of loneliness and isolation. They are very easy to identify. Name it for what it is. Call it what it is and allow Holy Spirit and the presence of YHVH to work in your life.

When I was a new born again Christian I would come into a crowd of people and I would not speak to anybody. If anybody was to approach me I would look at the ground so I would not connect with them. It was a spirit that at that stage had captivated and caught my soul, but as I began to identify its habit patterns and its power I found that there were some things that I could use to break its hold.

When that spirit would come to me and say, "They don't want to speak to you anyway; they're not really interested in you," immediately I would start to withdraw from people. That withdrawal is drawing away from connection with the people who can help, where you can meet and have meaningful relationship, instead of connecting in a relationship with a demonic spirit that drives you. Then I would feel self-hatred and I would think, "Man why am I doing this? I hate myself when I do that." Have you ever said that? That is the work of a familiar spirit.

Then I would begin to feel ashamed of the way I responded because I hated myself. How can I hate myself when my Father loves me? And the familiar spirit would say, "Well, how can He love you if you hate yourself? Don't you know you're supposed to love yourself?" And so the pattern would continue.

Then I would go to things like feeling sorry but without true repentance because I did not know what I was dealing with. So I would come to the place of feeling remorse and then say, "Father I thank You that somehow I can walk free of this thing," not really repenting but coming to an emotional place and just going through a cycle of religious works. The next time the same process starts all over again with thoughts and fantasies of dreaming of the potential.

It is like the cycle of violence that is in a man's life when in an abusive situation; he will go through exactly the same things because the spirit of violence is a familiar spirit to him that makes him behave in a certain sin cycle.

False Altars

I am one of those people who loves to have pictures to work with in the spirit. I have got this secret place in the spirit realm that the Lord and I go and meet together. One day when I was finished communing with the Lord in that place, as I came out of that place, across from me in the spirit was this other high place with an altar on it and inside of me I got really offended. I said, "How dare somebody in the spirit set up an altar to a demon spirit right where I commune and connect with YHVH?" The Lord said to me, "You put it there."

We have familiar spirits in the high places of our soul. Whenever we go into a sin cycle we are making a sacrifice in that high place of our life to that demon spirit that destroys the anointing and increase from glory to glory in the Lord.

I understand that there are valley experiences that the Word says can become a place of life (Isaiah 41:18) because the valley is where the life is. But when people go into the valleys and experience death and destruction, heartache and pain, they often find that familiar spirits that are in the high places are controlling the walk through the valley places. If you are having a hard time it may be because you have demon spirits connected to your soul in the high places and you have never torn down the idols and the altars out of the spirit realm.

We are spirit beings and altars must be torn down in the spirit realm. You cannot just think about it, you must actively name those things and tear down the places inside your spirit where you have made sacrifices to those demonic spirits.

The next time I went up to that high place of communion with YHVH in the spirit realm I went across and kicked that other altar down. These sin patterns form a path in the spirit to the place of sacrifice so you have to build a new path of connectedness with YHVH, tearing down that altar and building a new place of communion. Then that place becomes a place of connection with YHVH instead of connection with a demon spirit. It is hard work, it does not just go "click" and you are free from it. You need to crucify the flesh habit pattern, speaking and decreeing into that spirit power and breaking its hold and influence, so that YHVH can bring you into a place of communion. Sometimes I found I would be halfway round that sin cycle before I would recognise that I was in it. But with every one of those there is another pathway off it to the place of encounter with YHVH.

"But remember this — the wrong desires that come into your life aren't anything new and different. Many others have faced exactly the same problems before you. And no temptation is irresistible. You can trust God to keep the temptation from becoming so strong that you can't stand up against it, for he has promised this and will do what he says. He will show you how to escape temptation's power so that you can bear up patiently against it" (1 Corinthians 10:13 TLB).

I purposed in the spirit realm to begin to build a place of encounter with YHVH and so, instead of being a loud voice inside of me, the familiar spirit became a pursuing voice that was on the outside of me. Then I set up boundary lines in the spirit of love, joy and peace, and when I felt those voices begin to assail those boundary lines I would not allow them access to my spirit. We are spirit beings and we function in the spirit world. We are able to exert pressure on the spirit world to bring change, to influence our lives to Godliness.

Provocative Looks

I find that when a young person dresses or acts provocatively, it can be a familiar spirit related to rejection saying inside of them, "I want people to look at me so I feel good" or, "Do that because it will make you feel good." There is nothing wrong with looking attractive, but what are the voices behind it? Deal with the voice and then the person that is within will begin to show on the outside.

We need to realise that YHVH wants to enable and equip us to overcome as Jesus says, *"...In Me you may have [perfect] peace. In the world you have tribulation and distress and suffering, but be courageous [be confident, be undaunted, be filled with joy]; I have overcome the world." [My conquest is accomplished, My victory abiding.]"* (John 16:33 AMP). We need to wage a personal war against these spirits, their function and their operation around our lives. Usually I have found there are certain areas in the lives of believers where these cycles are present. We must see them as a personal adversary to our life in God. Once started on this path the battle can often become quite intense with the cycles increasing and becoming more frequent. If this occurs, I have found that one on one personal confession aids in destroying these cycles and the power and hold of these familiar spirits over our lives and is of great benefit to us.

Contending against these Spirits

We must see a familiar spirit as a somebody, not just a something that is in the ethereal world out there somewhere. It is a spirit being that does not have a body to express itself through and therefore it uses you to express itself to the world around you. It is an entity. When you can identify the emotion, you can name the entity, its character, its personality, and its traits.

When you can identify clearly, you can go to war clearly. I want to teach you to be very sharp in the way you pray, not using a great big broad bat and trying to break through something. The sharper it is the easier it is going to go through. The more specifically we pray, the more YHVH is licensed to move on our behalf. When you are praying about these things you need to be very sharp and very specific in the way you contend with them, fighting in the spirit and contending against their control, decreeing into them and breaking the power of the sin cycle. You need to actively war against these things in the spirit to tear them down. We must take the Word in the spirit realm and enforce the judgment of God against those things that rule against us because it is God's judgment that breaks the power of sin and death in our lives and it is God's righteousness that births us into life.

Possessing the Land

The good thing about it is, once you go in and you spoil that strongman, the Word says you take him captive and spoil all his goods. That means you can run over everything he has ever done and throw away the rubbish, make a new connection and a new place and allow Holy Spirit to become your strong man. This is something you need to apply in the spirit. I ask Holy Spirit to become my strong man, to become the gate keeper of my spirit, soul and body, so that no demon spirit can abide in the gates of my spirit, soul and body (see my Gateways of the Three-Fold Nature of Man manual). I speak very specifically into the gates of my spirit, soul and body so that Holy Spirit will become the gate keeper. This is because where He is gate keeper, demonic spirits cannot sit. But you must go in. The Word tells us YHVH said to Israel, *"be strong and go in and take possession of the land" (Deuteronomy 11:8 AMP).* The Word *possess* actually means to dispossess that which is already there. Do not allow circumstances and the seeming great weight of the thing to encompass and shut your soul down.

We need to work through the process of confession, identifying clearly our body, soul and spirit gates that are personally shut or accessed by these spirits. Our soul gates are conscience, reason, imagination, mind, emotions, choice and will. Our body gates are the eye gate (sight), ear gate (hearing), mouth gate (taste), nose gate (smell) and feel gate (touch). I would find out which areas of my gateways had been accessed by these spirits. Sometimes you know when you are going to the shops or you are walking down the street and you get a whiff of a fantastic smell and think, "Oh I really would like that". It is a familiar spirit of gluttony. Call it what it is! There is a voice inside of you saying, "Wouldn't that taste nice?" It has attached to your nasal passages, which stimulate the desire for something inside your bloodstream and release chemicals that make your stomach grumble and you think, "Yeah, I would love that." So if you are addicted to food and addicted to those smells of food that drive you, it is because there is a familiar spirit sitting on the nasal gateway of your life that shuts you down, that gets into your conscience and blocks your conscience from knowing that it is wrong to respond to food like that. One way to break that kind of thing is to go on a fast. That will soon tell you what devils are hanging around your life.

It is similar with unclean spirits. When a person's life is connected to an unclean spirit, all they have to do is walk past a shop and they will see a picture and the thing in their eyes will go, "Wow, look at that!" Inside of them they are feeling, "No, No, No, No!" But the thing inside them says, "You'll enjoy that. No one will see, no one will know." It is actually a familiar spirit connected to the eye gateway that drives them and pushes them to look at pornography.

We need to understand that we are spirit beings and we have authority to take dominion over these things.

Battles are won by one victory at a time. Keep the focus and get each victory and then when you have that victory go on to the next one, and the next one, and the next one, and allow the cry to arise inside of you, "I want my land back!" You must possess your soul under the hand of YHVH and subdue it.

One of the roots that I have identified is the need to be loved by others, the need to be accepted by others and the need to be needed by others. Now there is nothing wrong with those when they are in God. But when they become an inordinate desire and the voice of the familiar spirit is a driving thing that we have to be needed by others and we will do anything to be needed by others including coming into a place of adultery, coming into the place of fantasy, lust, you name it, it is the drive that is indicative of a demon spirit attachment to our souls.

YHVH wants to bring us to liberty so that we can walk free from the bindings of these spirits and be free to express the power and the life of YHVH in the spirit world around us. It is familiar spirits in the house of God operating over the lives of people that have caused so many men of God to fall into adultery. Now I am not afraid of praying with women, but if I am going to get in a one on one counselling situation with a woman I either have my wife or one of the other people in the body that I am mentoring to stand with me so that there are two that can be a witness.

Be wise but do not be afraid of the spirit world; we have dominion over it. So many of us back away from the demonic and the spirit realm because we fear that maybe the devil is bigger than we are. We have more power as sons of God than the biggest demon has ever got inside its life, but because of the fear of the enemy many people have drawn away from spiritual warfare.

Seated in Heavenly Places

There has been a major focus on territorial spirits. That is a layer underneath celestial spirits. YHVH wants us to exert His dominion over those celestial beings. I call them governing spirits over territories, I mean like half of the United States. One of these spirits sits over Los Angeles; I have seen it, a celestial demon spirit. Not a terrestrial or territorial spirit. The ecclesia goes from revelation to revelation and in the place of revelation that YHVH is bringing us to very shortly, I believe that as a body internationally, there are going to be men and women who will be able to stand in the spirit in that realm and depose the thing that has controlled the river that is supposed to flow out of this arena. YHVH wants the body of Christ to rise to that place of dominion and I do not mean that it is a place of pride. It is a place of establishing that seat of authority. God's Word says we are seated in heavenly places (Ephesians 2:6). A heavenly place is a celestial place where the dominion of the Kingdom of God is exerted. The Word says we are seated in Christ. The Word also says, we wrestle not against flesh and blood, but against principalities and powers, wicked spirits and demon spirits in these heavenly places (Ephesians 6:12). It is the same realm but I believe it is YHVH who has kept that realm hidden from us because the ecclesia has not been ready to come to that place of sonship yet, but it is starting. Hear it from a prophet – it is starting in the body of Christ.

When I see what YHVH is doing and Holy Spirit is doing then I know what He is working on and what He wants to bring the ecclesia to. Instead of going into the city it takes me two or three days to begin to feel the wings of Holy Spirit and what He is working on in the spirit realm and what He wants to establish to bring the ecclesia to next. YHVH wants positional authority of dominion and He is doing a fast work in His kingdom to bring us to the place of dominion so we can take authority over these spirits that have exerted dominion over the realms of the natural world.

When you change the spirit realm you will change the natural realm. I do not even worry about the natural realm. As far as I am concerned it is in ignorance. It is something that is totally subject to the spirit realm. That is why, as spirit beings, we need to get in the spirit and work from the spirit realm over the earth. If you change the spiritual, you will change the natural.

I want to teach this to give you an idea of how to pray. That was my wife's idea. My wife is a very practical lady, and she says "You must give these people something to work with and pray into."

Well the first thing to do is recognise that we have an issue. Each one of those areas of the cycle I would speak into, I would decree its power broken. I would decree it cleansed by the blood of Jesus. I would decree it crucified in the cross and in Christ Jesus. I would destroy it with the Word of God, praying strongly in tongues to dismantle and smash the altar that I had set up, which would be right in the middle of that sin cycle where I would unknowingly be making the sacrifice to this demon; I would depose it out of its place of authority in my life (see Courtroom of God chapter in Realms of the Kingdom Vol.1).

Finally, the Word says, *"If we walk in the light as He Himself is in the light, we have fellowship with one another and the blood of His Son Yeshua purifies us from all sin"* (1 John 1:7 TLV).

Deliverance is only five percent of the work. The other ninety five percent is the restoration of the broken breaches in your life, where you must take up your cross and crucify that flesh nature inside of you. Deliverance breaks the drive, but it is the cross that breaks the need. The demon spirit drives and makes you desire something with an inordinate affection, but it is the cross that breaks the need for it so you can crucify those needs. Come before the Father and ask Him to identify and show you the areas that familiar spirits are attached to your life. Take that cycle of prayer illustrated above so that you can see the kind of thing I work with and work with the familiar spirits until you have clearly identified all your sin patterns and then go to war on them. If you find you cannot get victory over your sin patterns, go and confess them to somebody else who can stand with you and take authority over the spirit that drives you. Sometimes I find that you can dispossess a spirit power by doing strong warfare over it in your own soul. But sometimes you need someone to stand with you so that you two agree, and so just ask Holy Spirit, "Lord, what do You want me to do?" Then go to war.

Activation

Father I ask that the Word would have stripped bare and naked the attachments of familiar spirits in the lives of each person reading this. Lord I ask that Your Spirit and Your anointing would come in with fire Lord, with glory and anointing and begin to enable these men and women to stand up in the spirit to contend for their souls. My God, I ask that in the spirit world the battle would begin to finally go for them. Father, in the spirit world I hold the rod of authority, the rod of iron, the rod of dominion up in the spirit over these things in their lives, so that as they begin to discover them that they will find access ways to be able to build a place of communion and connection with Your presence and intimacy in Jesus name. Amen.

CHAPTER 4

DEALING WITH SPIRITUAL ATTACK

YHVH is doing things on the face of the earth that are really different from our past experiences. He really wants to change us and create in us a new heart, *"I will give you a new heart and put a new spirit within you"* (Ezekiel 36:26 NKJV), so that He can release His heart onto the face of the earth through us. YHVH is about to change everything in and through us.

Because of sin, the heavens were realigned to the chaos that Satan is in. It is our job to realign the heavens and bring them back into the divine order that YHVH created them in.

"I consider that the sufferings of this present time (this present life) are not worth being compared with the glory that is about to be revealed to us and in us and for us and conferred on us! For [even the whole] creation (all nature) waits expectantly and longs earnestly for God's sons to be made known [waits for the revealing, the disclosing of their sonship]... That nature (creation) itself will be set free from its bondage to decay and corruption [and gain an entrance] into the glorious freedom of God's children" (Rom 8:18-19, 21 Amp).

With the knowledge of all that the Father has done, when you begin to understand the full truth of what the devil tried to do, it will give you such a hatred for him and everything that he stands for that whenever Satan shows up you will just want to crush him! The devil tried to take away our inheritance – his job was to kill it, rob it and take it from us so that we would have nothing and he would have everything. *"The thief comes only in order to steal and kill and destroy..."* (John 10:10 AMP).

When it says that *"...the sons of God saw the daughters of men, that they were beautiful; and they took wives for themselves of all whom they chose"*

(Genesis 6:2). The sons of God were in the first creation; God created sons, male and female in one body. That is why they left their first estate (Jude 1:6) – they wanted to be able to make a name for themselves, because there was a greater inheritance in this arena than in their arena. The first time that God separated male and female from one body was when He took Eve out of Adam (Genesis 2:22) and the Kingdom of the Earth was made.

When the son or daughter of a Hebrew family married a Gentile, after the bride and bridegroom had come out of the huppah, they would take diamond, gold and sapphire dust and throw it over the bride and bridegroom as the power of endowment and their acceptance and sanctification of the marriage. Did you wonder why gold, diamonds, sapphires and precious stones are showing up? The Father has just gone 'whoosh' – "I sanctify the marriage of my Son to You". "...*And as the bridegroom rejoices over the bride, So shall your God rejoice over you*" (Isaiah 62:5 NKJV). I have five or six of these stones. They can come out of our body, or show up on the floor, they get dropped by angels as the Kingdom opens up and fall out of the realm of the spirit. Gold dust shows up. Why? Because the Father *can* do that- that is just who He is. The streets of Heaven are blue and they are paved like gold, transparent gold "...*They saw the God of Israel. And there was under His feet as it were a paved work of sapphire stone, and it was like the very heavens in its clarity*" (Exodus 24:10 NKJV). In its purest form, if you hold gold up to the sun, it is transparent. In comparison, the gold here on earth is junk; pure gold is a bluey colour; monatomic elemental gold is protein gold, it is gold that has been broken down from a metal element into a protein element. That is what Adam was made out of and it is a conductor of light.

The New Jerusalem coming down from Heaven is going to sit in a gold ring. It is going to be placed in a marriage band around the atmosphere of the earth. "*Then I, John, saw the holy city, New Jerusalem, coming down out of heaven from God, prepared as a bride adorned for her husband*" (Revelation 21:2 NKJV). It will be up there and you will see it but only those who have walked the way of the Kingdom will be able to ascend into it. If you do not learn how to ascend now, you will never learn how to ascend then. I have seen the New

Jerusalem, it is wonderful, it is a fantastic thing, it sits on a rock with many different layers of precious stones; it is just amazing.

There are secrets that YHVH is unlocking from the angelic arena that were ours, and YHVH is bringing them to the face of the earth.

I had a very interesting angel come into my room one night and he just happened to leave a feather behind. It was really amazing; I have seen them once or twice before – the angels that bring these circular feathers are all about government. I have seen them white and blue, and there are some pink ones as well. Our God is an amazing God. He does little things just to say, "Hey, this is real, this is not just some imaginative trip that we are going on".

The veil between the natural world and the spirit world is getting thinner and things are starting to manifest out of the spirit world. It is wonderful but it has got to happen: the world has got to see that YHVH is God and He is Lord – so He is going to do amazing things.

This angel came and talked to me about a whole lot of governmental things in the realm of the Kingdom, Heaven, how it all functions and how we govern out of Heaven; the protocols of the Kingdom and manifestations of government on the earth – as it is in Heaven onto the earth (Matthew 6:10). It was a very good conversation that lasted a couple of hours and I woke up in the morning and there was that feather sitting on my bed -thank you Jesus!

Displacing the Kingdom of Darkness
I want to look at dealing with spiritual attack; I have already taught on how to build a strong spirit in Realms of the Kingdom Volume 1, so if attack starts to happen you can stand up in your spirit and begin to deal with the thing that comes around you. When the demonic spirit world sees the glory begin to rest on a person, it will try to shut the light down. Demons know that if they can shut the light down they will shut you out of the Kingdom and stop that light shining. Light displaces darkness so they want darkness and not light because they all know that they came out of darkness.

The Bible says, *"My people are destroyed for lack of knowledge..."*

(Hosea 4:6). It is not for lack of knowledge of the demonic world that we are destroyed – there is so much knowledge of the demonic world. It is for lack of knowledge of the realm of the Kingdom that we risk being destroyed. We do not understand the Kingdom that we have inherited: the power, the dominion, the authority, the righteousness, the holiness, the purity and the sanctification of that Kingdom. We do not understand, and because we lack knowledge of those things, we get destroyed.

There is wrestling in you when you start extending the borders of your tent pegs, (Isaiah 54:2-5), because the demonic world knows that if you lift your tent pegs up and stick them out there, they have lost that much more room. They do not like losing kingdom, so they will do everything they can to make you focus on them. I have learned to turn deeper into the Kingdom and practise Kingdom realities more, because that will displace the demonic. Once I have done that, I then step out of that and now, "I bind you in Jesus' Name". I do not try to bind them and deal with the demonic world until I have gone into the Kingdom. This is a weighty revelation – I do not try to deal with the demonic realm until I have gone into Heaven, because without going into Heaven you have no glory. The only way you can deal with the demonic world, which is darkness, is out of the glory, because the glory is light, *"The light shines in the darkness, and the darkness has not overpowered it"* (John 1:5 TLV).

YHVH is wanting to transition us out of our engagement with iniquity, because whatever the eye hooks into multiplies. YHVH wants to draw us away from the garbage we are used to feeding ourselves (Matthew 5:29), and engage us into the Kingdom so that it becomes something that is so lodged and entrenched within us that we live out of that arena. Then once we live out of the Kingdom arena we can stand in this fallen arena and bring divine order to it. When you have been in Heaven, you step out of the realm of the Kingdom, step into this world and all that is there exudes in power out of your life, with spirit beams of glory light coming out of your body.

The devil does not want you to live as a son, he wants you to live in the record of what you have been, not who you are eternally. This present age is what you are made in, it is not who you are. Who you are is there in Heaven. As I am in the Father (John 14:20) I am in Heaven; as I live out of that arena I am in Heaven and I live out of the power of that arena. It is the lack of the knowledge of that which destroys me; but the enemy has got us to focus on the lack of knowledge of the demonic structures of the world and the systems of the demonic realm instead.

Ignorance of the mandate of Heaven over your life, ignorance of the power of the Kingdom manifesting through your life and ignorance of the glory that we are supposed to walk in is what causes us to be destroyed. If we have the power of the mandate of YHVH, and we are fully aware of who we are and what we stand in, it will be revealed in everything we do.

The Kingdom realm is very important for us to understand, *"Lest Satan should take advantage of us; for we are not ignorant of his devices"* (2 Corinthians 2:11). The word 'devices' can also be translated 'purposes, thoughts and intents'. A device can also be a covert operation against a believer. The devil's thoughts and intents are to stop you engaging Heaven; his devices are to stop you going there, therefore you feel unholy and unrighteous. The devil does not want you to go there because he knows that the moment you turn up there you are going to be made clean (Zechariah 3:5) and then he will have no power over your life. The greatest thing we can talk about and engage is the Kingdom of God. We must go into the Kingdom, because in the Kingdom is our rest, and out of that place of rest comes the government of YHVH in our lives. Then there is a place for that government to sit on our lives and then to manifest through us into the world around us, to bring that government onto the face of the earth.

You Will Become Like Whatever You Look at

We have looked at the enemy too much and whatever you look at you become like – why look into the darkness?

One thing I really love about the Kingdom realm is that once you learn to go in and out of it you can engage it and it does not take long. It is a pathway; everything in the realm of the spirit is about a pathway – a learned process. The way you learn in the natural arena is the same way you learn about the things of the spirit. YHVH is wanting us to unlearn the garbage we have learned and to learn a new pathway. I used to live in Africa as a little child; we did not have TV in those days in Africa, so we used to make our own amusements. One of the most entertaining things we would do was to find the pathway the Africans were using up a hillside. I had no idea why the pathways go 25 metres this way and 25 metres that way, when it is only 3 metres to the top – I could never figure that out. So we used to take a little hoe and remove the grass, change the path and put stones in the old path. Then we would watch locals coming along. It was hilarious – their brains were so used to the old path that you would see a few of them walking around the stones. Finally they would get the idea that it was shorter this way and they would start using the new path, so the grass grew over the old path as though it had never been there. It is like that in the spirit; we have got to learn new pathways. We need to make new pathways for the neurons in our brains to be able to hold and function out of the realm of the Kingdom and the things of the glory of God. We need to have our mind renewed *"…Be transformed from the inside out by renewing your mind. As a result, you will be able to discern what God wills…"* (Romans 12:2 VOICE). Having our mind renewed means making new neuron pathways in our brain that agree with the realm of the Kingdom instead of the world that we live in and the processes of learning we have been born into.

We are snared in the record of what we are made in – our parents' image. *"…That they may come to their senses and escape the snare of the devil, having been taken captive by him to do his will"* (2 Tim 2:26 NKJV).

A snare can also mean a trap or a strategy set by the enemy to capture you and keep you captive or to make you a prisoner of war. In the next chapter I want to teach about the devil's trophy room, where we can go and get back what has been stolen from our lives, hallelujah!

Ascent into the Glory

"For we do not wrestle against flesh and blood, but against principalities, against powers, against the rulers of the darkness of this age, against spiritual hosts of wickedness in the heavenly places" (Eph 6:12 NKJV). Spiritual attack can happen when something that is seated in a heavenly

place tries to override your dominion. You must first ascend and then you can descend. Spiritual attack comes as the enemy tries to override your authority and as you bring that authority or mandate he tries to remind you of your sin. How weak, how vulnerable and how pathetic you are as a little worm with human DNA sitting inside of you, instead of the glorious creature manifesting YHVH inside of you, that you are called to be in Christ.

So he tries to stop us being mandated by YHVH, manifesting the glory of the presence of YHVH around us, to shut our open heaven; he tries to close it down, but the way to keep an open heaven is to go up again. Then you come down again, and every time you are in the glory presence you take your swords.

Satan was made as a covering cherub; and music is important to the demonic realm. They use it because of who Satan was: he had all the instruments and the capacity in his being to be able to make music. The Bible talks about the pipes and timbrels that were in his being: *"You were in Eden, the garden of God; Every precious stone was your covering...The workmanship of your timbrels and pipes was prepared for you on the day you were created"* (Ezek 28:13 NKJV).

This talks about these things actually in his being; he did not have to play an instrument, he *was* the instrument. We do not have to make anything, we already are the thing. It is empowering to understand this – I do not have to try to become something, I already am. If I am in Christ, I am in the Father (John 14:20), therefore I already am invited to manifest His glory. When Moses asked, who shall I say sends me? *"...God said unto Moses, I AM THAT I AM..."* (Ex 3:14 KJ2000). As I am there, I am here. Because I am in YHVH, when the spirit world sees me, they see 'I am that I am.' So when people say to me, "who are you?" I am that I am. When the spirit world comes to you, you say, "I am that I am." Two different patterns, so when you present yourself in the world, you are a gate of eternity because Jesus is the gate (John 10:9) and I am like Jesus: Jesus is the first born of many who are just like Jesus (Rom 8:29). We carry the same realm of eternity He does, because the Bible says YHVH puts eternity inside our hearts (Ecc 3:11). So you have an arena to the whole of eternity that sits inside of you and you are a gate for people to see the realm of eternity. As I am here, I am there, because when people see me here fully manifesting eternity, I am there.

When the spirit world comes around me, I go into 'I am that I am.' Now that is power, if you can get that revelation and work on it. I have spent days over months meditating around this stuff, standing there praying, "Father I thank you that I am that I am: as it is in Heaven, so it is upon the earth; as I am in You, You are in me; as You are in me, I am in You; as it is in Heaven, so it is on earth." Again, this is a pathway to learn engaging the Kingdom. The more you learn that pathway, the easier it gets for the glory to manifest around your life. The more you engage it, the glory begins to manifest around you and the spirit world sees the shift of time and space happening as you step outside of time and space and it goes "crack!" You step outside of time and space and stand as a supernatural spiritual being in the natural world. Now that is power; and if you want power, you do not just ask for it, you go and you become it, because Jesus has already said, *"All authority has been given to Me in heaven and on earth. Go therefore..."* (Matt 28:18-19 NKJV). So He has fully endowed us with the complete power to be in this natural world and step outside of time and space to become a supernatural spiritual being in the realm of the spirit. Then you can see the whole of your nation, because you are stepping outside of time and space. You can see the whole of the realm of the Kingdom and what is going on in the face of the earth; you can step up outside of it and you see the whole moving of the face of the earth, although you can be here in the natural world and yet totally absent to where you are. You step into another arena: you step into the Father because He is outside of time and space; you step into the reality of the glory of His Kingdom, therefore the whole of this world. The Bible says Adam was given dominion over the whole world, *"Then God said, "Let Us make man in Our image, according to Our likeness; let them have dominion...over all the earth..."* (Gen 1:26 NKJV). That means Adam could hold the whole earth inside his spirit man; Adam could encompass the whole realm of the spirit and take the whole sphere of the earth into himself. This is one issue to spend time cogitating and meditating over. We have got to turn the cogs inside our spirit being to engage the truth of the reality of what YHVH wants to bring us.

We have tried to coin some new words to describe the Kingdom realms, because the earthly vocabulary that we use does not describe some of the heavenly stuff. If you can get the reality of what I am talking about – as I am in Heaven so I am on the earth – then your life will change, because you will see yourself in Heaven and so you will walk in Heaven on the earth; and you will walk out of Heaven into the earth. So whenever you move, Heaven slides into time and space there with you; as Jesus says, "...*I am with you...*" (Matt 28:20 NKJV).

People say, "Jesus was casting out demons the other day...Jesus was healing." No – *you* were doing it, it is your spirit that is doing it, but Jesus is with you. He is not doing it, you are doing it, He has given you dominion to go and do it. Jesus is not going to do it, He has already done it; He is now telling you to reveal that. You become Jesus on the earth and you become a door of eternity (John 10:9).

One day I was dealing with some giants and trying to get to grips with who I was in the Kingdom realm.
The Lord just said, "Open your being."
I said, "What do you mean 'open my being'?"
He said, "You are a door of eternity, open your being and see what happens."

I can remember standing in that arena with all the Kingdom around me, mountains and the whole spirit realm; I could see the demonic world, which is the kingdom that Jesus was shown: "*The devil took Him up on an exceedingly high mountain, and showed Him all the kingdoms of the world and their glory*" (Matt 4:8). It does not say the kingdoms of the earth. Jesus was shown the kingdoms of the spirit world – whoever rules in the realms of the kingdoms of the spirit world rules on the face of the earth..

I have also wrestled with dragons in the earth and won. The reason I have won is because I know who I am and I have a legal right to go and do that.

The church has predominantly wrestled in one realm in all its warfare in the last 60-100 years and that is on the earthly plain. The Bible says, *"That at the name of Jesus every knee should bow, of those in heaven, and of those on earth, and of those under the earth"* (Phil 2:10 NKJV). The church has wrestled primarily with the things that are on the earth and we have wondered why we have never had lasting revival or seen the Glory of God manifesting. It is because we have never learned to wrestle with the things that are in heaven. I do not just mean in the atmosphere around the earth, that word 'heaven' means 'the celestial realm' and you and I can go there.

Under the earth is the other realm that has to bow the knee, and the only way it is going to bow the knee is if we go there. We as a church have usually only wrestled on one level and we have wondered why we have failed. I have been on a journey of discovery with some of these things but they are not taught because of religious disapproval.

When you have dealt with a dragon then you have got its lair. Everything in its lair is what is promised to the sons of God. It is called a trophy room of the devil – that is what dragons look after. You and I have access to those trophy rooms, *"Or how can one enter a strong man's house and plunder his goods, unless he first binds the strong man? And then he will plunder his house"* (Matt 12:29 NKJV). You and I need to go and take back those things promised to us and many of those things are in the earth. They are displayed to the kingdom in darkness as a trophy. The devil likes taking them out and I wait for when he brings them out because then it is even easier to get hold of them. (See the chapter entitled "The Trophy Room of the Devil."

I had a wrestle with a dragon that was at a volcano some time ago with some prophetic leaders. The mountain was puffing away and they were saying it was going to blow again. I said, "No it won't, I have an appointment with it." I went up there, got in the spirit and went into the volcano. I have met the dragon that was there two or three times and it has now become very quiet. You need to understand that we win.

The purpose of demonic attack is to derail us, to immobilise us and destroy our walk with YHVH and our service for Him. Whenever you find desire for YHVH and the love of YHVH dwindling in your heart, you may be under spiritual attack. Whenever you find yourself starting to move into a religious system of doing things and not a relationship of being, you may be under spiritual attack. People reject the ways of Heaven and get entangled with the ways of men, rejecting the glory, and replacing it with a system. This may make us feel better, and look like we are living a better life, but our works are like filthy rags anyway, it is not going to bring the Kingdom in a greater measure of manifestation.

One of the enemy's ways of attack is when he comes and confronts you, standing in front of you and trying to block you and tell you that you are not worthy to go into Heaven, asking you, "Who do you think you are? What right do you think you have to go in before the Father? – You sinned last night!" One of the things YHVH said to me was, "If you have done it 0.01% son, you have sinned, so just confess it and get it right." Sin, to a Hebrew is not the good and the bad we know with the Greek classification system that says one sin is worse than another. Sin, to a Hebrew, is anything that is not as it should have been, as it was before the fall – it changes the way you see yourself.

I live out of the Kingdom, so when the enemy says, "You have done this", I say, "Yes I have and I stand in Your presence right now Lord Jesus and confess it," because when I go there He makes me clean. (See "Courtroom of God" in Realms of the Kingdom Volume 1). We need to go there to get clean. With all our brownie points, trying to do the will of YHVH here, striving to *do the dos* and not to do the *don'ts*, when you do the *don'ts* more than you do the *dos*, you end up in a big mess because when you do not know what you *are*, you become a 'human doing' instead of a human being. You do not get clean this side of the glory. The only place you get clean is when you go into the Kingdom, and the pathway you learn is going in by faith – when you step in by faith, you become clean.

So when the enemy tries to stand in front of you and derail your going in, as he says, "You are not worthy, you are a sinner," the best way to deal with that is to say, "Yes I am. That is why my Father gave me Jesus – would you like me to remind you about what Jesus is to you in the end? I am now fully righteous in Christ

– I have that full power. Let's go and take you back in time and then forward in time and show you what you are going to be like when you burn shall we? Come with me." It is called putting him into his own snare – when he reminds you of what you are, you remind him of the future: that we are going to judge him and judge all those that fell with him, *"Do you not know that we shall judge angels?"* (1 Corinthians 6:3 NKJV). The devil is going to burn and he is not going to exist anymore. He will be finished, he will be a nothing. As he reminds me of myself, it does not worry me, because when I step into YHVH's presence I become His son. So when the accuser reminds you about what you are, you remind him about the future: "Let me prophesy into the spirit world – devil you are a nothing!"

That locks an arena of the Kingdom, it is called power and eternity; how can I describe this? If you were to take eternity and display it in the natural sense, what you would see is a complete distortion of everything as it goes into a spinning spiral – that is what a black hole is. It spins like that and when you step into eternity you become a black hole to the enemy where there is no end for him to ever get out. When you step into Heaven and then step down here, you become his judgement, because he sees his end in you.

When you engage that reality, standing in the realm of the spirit and the enemy comes to you, just stand – go into the glory, come out and open up the door of eternity here, because the Bible says YHVH puts eternity into a man's heart (Ecc 3:11). Therefore it is inside of me, I am just going to reveal it; so I reveal the realm of eternity and the enemy sees the whole distortion of his end manifesting. So you walk around in the spirit showing the demonic their end and when you turn up they think, "Oh no, who is going to die today?" You can walk across the face of the earth in the realm of the spirit, manifesting the Kingdom and showing the demonic spirit world that there is a son who is going to decree their end. Do not just talk about it – reveal it.

Sieges and blocks are another way that the devil comes against us: often he will lay siege to an area in your personal life, where you have really struggled with issues and you find you have a repetitive failure that you go back to in sin just feeling defeated. One of the things I have learned is that in the middle of your struggle, the Lord is looking you in the face saying, "I love you, and not only do I love you, but I am going to be with you in the middle of what you are doing; and if you will turn to Me and step into Me, I have made a way of escape for you because I will make you righteous and this thing will fall off your life." In the middle of your struggle, all you have to do is just turn, step in, receive the garment of righteousness, step out and that righteousness is over your life; you will then find that thing will just die. It is an amazing way to deal with repetitive sin because it is not full of 'don't do this' and the disciplines of trying not to do those things.

When you get into ministry you have got to be wise with what you do, but if any temptation comes out of the spirit world, then you step into the Kingdom and bring the Kingdom back into that temptation, and then you see the power of it dissipate. The more it persists, the more you go in. When you come back, if it is still there, you go in again. Then you step back here and release the glory and the power of YHVH against it. Then you become a siege against that thing and you start making ground against it, so you stretch the borders of your tent. Then there comes boundary lines around your life of love, joy and peace, and the conflict is right out there instead of being in here. In the same way as you have three skins and there are three layers in the atmosphere of the earth, there are three rings or layers you can establish as boundaries around your life: love, joy and peace. As you protect those boundaries, when the boundaries are being disturbed by the enemy you step into the realm of the spirit, right up to their boundaries and you confront them right in there, not out here, which takes the warfare right out of it.

Activation

Father we want to thank You today for Your Kingdom. Father, thank You that we are children of a Kingdom and of that Kingdom there will be no end.

We are rulers, kings and lords in the Kingdom, and You have made us Your sons. This is not an option Father, we are Your sons, we are seeded by You and because we are seeded by You we do not sin.

According to 1 John 3:9, "*Whoever has been born of God does not sin, for His seed remains in him; and he cannot sin, because he has been born of God.*"

Lord, because we are seeded by You we do not sin, because in the glory there is no sin. In the glory there is no power of sin, because the glory manifests and destroys the power of sin in us because of the cord of the DNA Jesus has given us.

Father, I ask that the reality of what I am teaching about would become the portion of these men and women reading it today, in the Name of Jesus. Hallelujah.

Chapter 5

The Devil's Trophy Room

I want to share some of my life experiences from a particular realm that YHVH has enabled me to uncover. This has been as a result of times when I know that I should have received something in the spirit that was blocked. There have been times when I have done a forty day fast and I have received nothing. By then I am worse off than I was when I started, because not only am I hungry and tired, but I am frustrated because I am sitting there with no answer out of Heaven about the issues in question. I can remember once about three weeks later, a flow of the glory started that I should have received when I was in the middle of my fast and it continued for forty days after that. I used to get really frustrated when things like that happened and I did not understand as I do now, which is a real shame because I realise that I missed out on so much. Nevertheless, out of some experiences the Lord began to give me, I started to realise that there was something more about what is happening in the spirit world. It was not just that I was not receiving something, but actually that something that I should have received was going somewhere else – somewhere it should never have gone to.

A Brother's Lost Mantle

I can remember one day being very grieved hearing about a man of God who had stood for many years and had been an inspiration, a lighthouse and a pillar in the house of the Lord worldwide, because I found out that he had fallen – things had occurred that should not have done. I can remember being grieved and one day just praying in the spirit and thinking, "Lord you know that what this man carried should have been passed onto someone else". Meditating around this whole thing, I probably spent eight hours just interceding and praying for this man and holding him in the spirit thinking, "Father, what happened?" I began to feel this tremendous loss for the body of Christ and I thought, "Lord, this should not be. This grief and loss should not have been allowed against the body of Christ, because the mantle this man had should have been passed on to the body". I can remember feeling such a sense of loss. Then the Lord graciously shifted me in the realm of the spirit, although I could not comprehend what I was seeing because I had no grid for it. I drew back and I thought, "Lord, I do not understand this, I need You to teach me."

The Lord began to teach me about the devil's trophy room, and I want to teach about it from my own experiences in this chapter. This is because it is important that we realise there are things that were purposed by YHVH to be released onto the face of the earth, around our lives and even some of our destinies that have been waylaid and have gone into a trophy room. Gifts and callings of YHVH never get erased, they always exist, but they can just be hidden.

I am going to share some of my visions on that journey with you because the greatest thing I know about visions we have is that they are doorways, windows of opportunity for us to go back into and experience in the time line. Yesterday is as today and tomorrow is as today in heavenly realms, so it does not really matter where you are in the spirit, because you are outside of time and space, and so you can still go in and experience the fullness of what happened yesterday as well as taking back what was lost.

I had an amazing vision that started me on a journey trying to figure out what the Lord had showed me. I began to look at historical documents and papers associated with the Word of God and how some of the kings behaved with one another when they conquered a nation.

The Defeated King as a Trophy

In ancient history, in some savage cultures, when a king conquered a nation he would take the other king captive. The conquering king's soldiers would then pluck out the defeated king's eyes so he could never see again and then strip him naked and cut off his private parts so that he was emasculated. They would take out his tongue, and sometimes they would cut off his thumbs or his hands so that he could never hold anything, or cut off his big toes or his feet so he could never walk again properly or be any kind of threat to them. After that they would put him in a caged wooden cart and parade him around the city or nation, showing him off as their trophy of defeat, like a chained animal. They would parade him through the streets of their nation as a victory prize, with all that belonged to that king now in the cart behind him, showing off all the spoils that they had won in war and giving the people a chance to throw rotten fruit and rubbish at this defeated king, who was now blind, but who used to run a nation.

It is amazing how the natural world takes on the timbre of the spirit world. I can remember hearing this noise one day as I was praying, and I was pursuing what the Lord was revealing to me and feeling, "Argh! No way. The devil is not going to do that." I can remember hearing this noise in the spirit world, and I became quite dismayed and concerned because it was a rejoicing in the kingdom in darkness. And I know there is no rejoicing down there because it is not a nice place to be. But I heard a kind of "Rah! Yes!" I was wondering what on earth it was when YHVH shifted me in the spirit and put me on a viewing platform over this arena. I saw a mantle being carried on a trophy cart in the spirit world. As I realised this, righteous anger began to grow inside of me and unfortunately, when I get mad I look for a fight. By this stage I was undone and I thought, "Lord, this has to change". The Lord then began to give me a scripture.

"When a strong man, fully armed, guards his own palace, his goods are in peace. But when a stronger than he comes upon him and overcomes him, he takes from him all his armor in which he trusted, and divides his spoils" (Luke 11:21-22).

In this scriptural account there is a house with lots of goodies in it with a strong man who guards that house full of goodies. The strong man can be defeated and then all that has been in that house becomes your possession. The word *overcome* in this passage in the book of Luke means to conquer, to prevail, to get victory over and to subdue, but its implication is "to smother". So, I decided, "Ok, well if I am a spirit being, then what I saw was in the spirit realm. The realm of the spirit is outside of time and space; that means yesterday is as today, which means I can go back into the spirit, into the door that was given to me to see what was going on, step in through that door, and begin to participate." The plan sounded pretty logical, so I spent a few days praying and fasting to get my heart focused in holiness before the Lord. This is because I did not understand at that stage that I could go there and then become holy, which means I could instantly go there anyway. But it is a good thing to fast anyway. So I spent a few days fasting and beginning to build an engagement and desire to begin to take back what had been stolen.

After spending some time praying I began to draw on the root call of the memory of the fullness of what I saw in the spirit when I was taken by the Lord into that vision. I began to desire to go after it because I had seen this beautiful mantle, sitting inside a caged room, being spat at by demons. This mantle had been taken down through a passageway into the earth, into the kingdom in darkness with great glee, gusto and rejoicing. I had become really mad because I recognised the mantle that they were carrying off was from this man who had fallen. I thought, "No way – you are not going to have this; you are not going to rob this from the body of Christ". At this stage I did not know what I know now. So I thought, "Well God, whatever it takes I am going after this thing, and I am going to take it and store it in my chamber until this brother either comes back restored, or somebody else comes into the kingdom and says, 'Father, where is this mantle?'"

I drew on the recall of the vision and entered back into the door. This time I stepped into the vision because a vision is a doorway of opportunity for your participation. If you do not go and participate in your vision, then actually all you do is have it as a wonderful looking experience and you never engage the Kingdom realms and the reality of the vision that YHVH wants to bring you into.

The Devil's Trophy Room

I stepped back into the vision and I found myself standing on this pathway and I was now beneath or inside the earth. I saw this cart disappear around the corner so I went after it. When I got round the corner I found myself in an amphitheatre that would house probably four to five hundred thousand demons, sitting around celebrating, mocking and delighting in the failure of a son who had fallen. They were now hitting his mantle and they were taking it off into a trophy room. I can remember coming around that corner and turning up in this trophy room but inside of me and around me I was not what I am used to looking at in the mirror, I was this cocoon of glory walking on lightning. Everything inside of me rose with righteous anger as I strutted through that amphitheatre with determination. After all, when a lion turns up among a herd of animals, who is afraid in that situation – the animals or the lion? Even though that lion is amongst a herd of animals that have the chance to destroy him, who has the fear?

I can remember as I walked through this arena it became amazingly silent. There was a terror that began to happen in that amphitheatre as the demons knew any one of them could be dead at any time, because the judgement of YHVH that you and I are able to wreak in that arena is tremendous. All you have to do is envelope yourself in who you are in the Kingdom, magnify that light in darkness and the darkness is dispersed as light destroys the darkness. At that moment I was a lamp burning in the amphitheatre, so they made a very wise choice to leave me alone. I can remember walking through that place with one objective: that mantle that was being carried down the passageway – I was going to have it. I set my heart and followed the cart.

The Dragon

The Bible says, *"Or how can one enter a strong man's house and carry off his property, unless he first ties up the strong man? Then he will thoroughly plunder his house"* (Matthew 12:29-30 TLV). I remember coming round this corner down to a doorway and in front of the doorway was a hulking great big dragon as tall as a two storey building in my eyes. The amazing thing was I was on its level. That seemed hard to understand when I am only a human body that is seemingly small, but when you are in the spirit you are not who you are in the natural world; and it was amazing to be eye to eye with this thing. It was probably one of the first times I had encountered a dragon in its arena in the earth and my hackles started rising as I was thinking, "I am a lion!" Looking at this thing looking back at me, with a big head, it had ominous looking teeth, but I knew that I have teeth as well and in Christ my teeth are bigger, my glory is bigger, the dominion I have is better, the power I have is stronger and the dominion and authority I have carries far more weight than that dragon. The Bible says, *"When a man of power with his full array of weapons guards his own palace, everything inside is secure. But when a new man who is stronger and better armed attacks the palace, the old ruler will be overcome, his weapons and trusted defences will be removed, and his treasures will be plundered"* (Luke 11:21-22 VOICE). Who is stronger, me or the dragon?

We live in fear of the things we do not understand. We think the demonic is stronger because they have been portrayed in the media as stronger, faster, better and more equipped. As I came around the corner the dragon challenged me, hissing through its teeth. Scriptures flickered through my mind like billiard balls bouncing around in my head. I started thinking, "Lord you have put me here. I am here with one objective – to get the mantle that was taken into that room". The Bible says when one stronger than he shall arrive or turn up, he shall overcome him. The word *overcome* means to smother; and for me there is only one way to smother darkness and that is with light. Just as Moses threw his rod down and it became a serpent I fired a challenge back at the dragon. As I did, a fine shaft of white golden thread shot out of my mouth that smothered its face, went around it and covered the whole thing's being, and it was crushed in this canopy of light. No big confrontation, just *a victory cry* out of my being – a representation of who I am

I now understood the Word which says, *"I pursued my enemies and destroyed them, And I did not turn back until they were consumed (eliminated)"* (2 Samuel 22:18 AMP) and *"God … will soon defeat satan and give you power over him [crush] satan under your feet"* (Romans 16:20 EXB).

Suddenly, not only did I smother him but the door was opened to me and I walked into a chamber of about a thousand metres long by five or six hundred metres wide and half a mile high, layered with crowns, sceptres, battle equipment, gold, silver, documents, scrolls, mantles and destinies. The whole thing was full of everything that should have been given to the sons of God; all these trophies, displayed and locked up, becoming inaccessible to the saints of YHVH until this day. But I had gone there with one objective – to get hold of this man's mantle, so that is what I went after. The spiritual realm is amazing: when you set your eye on something, it will begin to somehow call to you or manifest its presence. His mantle was there glowing so I picked it up and walked out of that trophy room and up into the realm of the normal arena that we live in here. I put his mantle into my mountain where I now have it hidden. I know there is going to come a day when that brother will call me and say, "Ian, you have got my mantle, can I have it back please?" That is going to be a good day!

On my way out of the trophy room the thought went through my head, "I wonder what is in there that belongs to me? I wonder what it has taken of mine?" When you have been to a place in the spirit realm you can go again because what you see you can inherit.

My Personal Trophy Room

So again I set my heart, but this time I was going after my inheritance. I did not know how much was down there. I just did not want the demonic realm to have my life. So I went back into the trophy room, but this time I did not have to go down that passage because I already had the anchor of where it sat and which room it was in, so I transitioned straight into the room. That is the greatest thing about the Kingdom: you do not have to walk the same path once you have gone somewhere; you can choose where you enter. I remember re-entering the arena, back into the room, and somehow, I knew there was a room, as I went in there, on the left hand side. It was like a vault that had these special things put inside it and I knew my things were stuck in there for some reason. When I got down inside this room I went to the left down inside the vault and there were my family's lives all written down. All my family tree and everything that was ever stolen from my family were shunted in these rows and rows of things. I said, "I will have some of that, thank you." A box that was stuck in this little hole contained drawers and drawers of things. I pulled this box out and there were papers inside there that should have been delivered to the earth, for me. There were destiny things that I should have inherited, that had been locked away and stolen by the enemy. There were testimonies of the glory and the manifestation of the glory in my generation that had been lied about to conceal who I was supposed to be here, so that satan could have me trained to be a sorcerer. Now, we see these things, but it is amazing, when you take something back you cannot carry it. There is one place it goes – into your belly. I thought, "I will fill my belly with the things of the kingdom" – *t*hings that belong to me that I should have had and I do not have because somebody in my family line gave them up. And so I started receiving them in the spirit and I felt pretty full by the time I left that place.

We are a nation called the sons of God, that have been given a mandated, equipped right as heirs to the government of YHVH to see and rob and take back all that has been stolen from our lives and our family's lives. Our problem is, we have never known where it has gone, so we have never known where to go to get it back. I began regular trips going down there. It is amazing, when a son of light turns up in darkness, darkness disappears and dissipates. The more you trespass and go in there, the more residue remains of the nature of what you carry in that atmosphere. And gradually it became lighter and lighter in there. The most amazing thing is I got inside there one day and found I was not the only person inside there, there were other people going in and out of that room and I was saying, "Yeah, yeah" – and then I thought "Oi! *That is mine!*" But hey, you have got to share amongst the brethren. I do not mind sharing those kinds of spoils. Just because I went in there first does not mean to say that I had the sovereignty and right to it all – it is for everybody.

The thing that fascinated me more than anything is that we have been told that darkness will remain in those places. But the only reason it stays there is because light has not been brought in there yet. We have been given a mandated opportunity by YHVH to take away darkness and replace it with light. We are children of light. Darkness cannot penetrate light. You can take the blackest of rooms, but light a match and the whole room will light up with the glory from just one match.

This is what happens in the kingdom that is in darkness. When you turn up and you reveal who you are to the supernatural world, the glory that is in you lights up the whole arena and there is terror in the ranks of the kingdom in darkness, because a son of light has turned up to take back what is rightfully his.

I do not go from this arena into that one. I go from here into the realm of Heaven. From the realm of Heaven I then walk into that arena that is in darkness, because it is all part of one kingdom. The kingdom is connected – two layers in darkness, the rest is light. So I walk from what I have seen and what I carry in the glory, into the darkness. I do not go from the darkness and the vulnerability of this world into the darkness of that demonic arena. I go from the glory light of my Father in Heaven into the darkness. It makes it so much easier. We wonder why people have been hurt in the church in spiritual warfare – because we have taught them to go and *hammer* into darkness from this arena, and because we have never taught them to go into the Kingdom of God.

The motive of the enemy in displaying what he has stolen is to intimidate, to demoralise, to de-motivate and to bring fear into minds and hearts: that if we do anything against this arena or this kingdom in darkness then we will be in trouble. He tried to do that with Jesus at the cross – to display Him before the world as a broken, destitute man hanging on the cross with no power. But Jesus said to His disciples, *"Or do you think that I cannot now pray to My Father, and He will provide Me with more than twelve legions of angels?"* (Matthew 26:53). Twelve legions of battle ready, warring, prepared angels at His bidding; that is a good army.

I have often wondered what happened to the revivals of the past. I often wondered what happened to believers who started off well and ended up in a mess – ministries and the glory that has been poured out onto the earth. Even in our day we have seen moves of YHVH start and then it is like a tap is turned off and they just finish. I often wondered what had happened to all that has been poured out. Guess where it all goes? It goes into the devil's trophy room. There have only been a very few times where I have seen in the spirit that the glory has been stopped by Holy Spirit because people have grieved Him.

The crowns that we have lost from our lives are often stored in trophy rooms, with the glory that we once had. Have you ever been ministering in a certain way and it is like one day something goes, *"Snap"* and you cannot get back to what it was like before. A lot of believers have experienced that. That happens because a crown has been removed from your head, and it is locked away in the spirit world somewhere.

The king, the president or the ruler of a kingdom always had a special place for the best gifts, the best trophies and the most valuable things. The demonic world has only tried to copy what is in Heaven. They cannot create anything of their own. What they do is invade what is there and create an environment so that they can try and duplicate and use what is not theirs as their own. The demonic world has no right to the supernatural world. It has no right to manifest and do the things that it wants to do. The reason it does it is because we do not stop it. The demonic world will always take the supernatural, pollute it, fill it with darkness, present it to the church and say, "You cannot do this!"

Before I got saved I was trained by demonic spirits how to become something that would be the church's worst nightmare. But YHVH had another plan and He has turned that around so I am now the devil's worst nightmare, and it is a pledge. I have this amazing relationship with the devil: I hate his guts, he hates mine, and I win! It is a very good understanding we exist by. So, I can remember going into my own trophy room and there were all these things in the drawer, so I took my drawer out and I walked out with it. When I came out I was able to see what I had lost and I actually grieved over those losses.

Our Trophy Rooms

In the body of Christ, many of us, not only in our own lives, but in our generations past, have lost many things to the enemy that have been taken into his trophy room. In that trophy room he has displayed spoils from our lives in victory to other demons to show them how weak and vulnerable you are. One thing I know about YHVH is the more we go into His presence, the more He makes new stuff. Now, not only did I have what I had lost but I had my new stuff, and the Bible says that *"The glory of this latter temple shall be greater than the former, says the L*ORD *of hosts"* (Haggai 2:9). YHVH has made what the devil took better, stronger, faster and more powerful than I could have had here, and the devil made a mistake in taking it away because not only did I get my inheritance back, but I have got interest back now as well.

One of the key things that unlocks the realm of the Kingdom of God for you and me is our entry into Heaven, because whatever you have lost will come back out of Heaven into your life. Not only that but it will be released around you, in a greater measure than you had before. The issue is you and I need to go there and get it.

I began to realise that YHVH not only wants us to have our inheritance back, but He also wants us to have back everything the enemy has stolen from us. The Bible says, *"For when satan, strong and fully armed, guards his palace, it is safe – until someone stronger and better armed attacks and overcomes him and strips him of his weapons and carries off his belongings"* (Luke 11:21-22 TLB). We can go and take back all his goods; everything he has becomes ours because we have overcome the strongman at the door.

You and I can go and fill that trophy room with glory and no demon can go back in there again (Isaiah 14:2). Now that is one trophy room out of an uncountable number. Each nation and each country has a trophy room, each family has a trophy room and each individual has a trophy room. The record of your family line has a trophy room with the same structure, the same demonic bondage and the same system of government of control. You know, for every family there is an angel, for every individual there is an angel, for every church there is an angel, for every city there is an angel, for every nation there is an angel, for every tectonic plate there is an angel, but no one ever talks about them. It is the same system of government. There are prince warring angels that are sitting over this nation, and over each city, waiting for the sons of YHVH to stand up and say, "We loose you to do your work, to fight for us and bring the Kingdom of God on the earth as it is in Heaven".

The reason there is rarely a move of the glory of God is because people have allowed the angels to be chained, never taking the time to ask YHVH about the angelic assignments in each place and release them. There have been angels over many, many churches that have never been loosed and released because we have never honoured them. John does exactly that, *"To the angel of the church of Ephesus write... And to the angel of the church in Smyrna write... And to the angel of the church in Thyatira write"* (Revelation 2:1, 8, 18). John writes to seven angels of these different churches in Revelation; this is in the Bible.

You have the capacity to speak to an angel and to begin to mandate it to deal with issues in church life. Some months ago I realised I had let an angel in my own church become bound, so I went and spoke to it, commanded it to be loosed and begin to manifest what it needs to do to bring the church into divine order. YHVH turned the church upside down because I mandated the angel to do its job. Angels are waiting for the sons of God to say, "Good to have you, welcome, I receive and honour your ministry, do what you have to do, manifest yourself and fulfil the destiny and mandate YHVH put on you in this place". The same is true in a family; you have an angel assigned to your family. You can mandate it, you can release it to do what it needs to do around and in your family life. You also have an individual angel assigned to your life. It is a warring angel that follows you everywhere. You can release and mandate it to fulfil its call in your life and help you fight. YHVH has given us all these things, but no one teaches about it, we are too busy naming the demons and we miss out on the whole angelic arena.

The first time I ever spoke to an angel that governs the tectonic plate, it stood seven or eight hundred feet high. These are not little babies. These are major warring angels that are waiting for the sons of God to release them to do the assignment that YHVH has commanded them to do. They have just been waiting there for years and years, waiting for someone who will rise up and say, "I am a son of God. I have been into Heaven. I have the scroll out of Heaven. Here is your fulfilment, go and do your work." Now that would start to change a lot of things if the church did that in Jesus' name.

God, in His Kingdom has a vision of *"...A bride in all her beauty [in splendor; glorious], with no evil or sin [stain or wrinkle]… but pure [holy] and without fault"* (Ephesians 5:27 EXB), a bride victorious in the provision of His Kingdom for their lives. It is time that you and I pursued, overtook and recovered all that has been stolen from the house of God. Why do you think the world has the gold? I am not saying go and chase the gold, but we need to overtake the spirit world that hides the gold from the house of God. Go and take it back, first in the spirit, then in the natural world. YHVH wants us to actually engage His kingdom; and I believe the command of YHVH is coming in the realm of the spirit for each of us individually to pursue, to overtake, and to recover all, as David did:

"David inquired of the LORD, saying, "Shall I pursue this troop? Shall I overtake them?" And He answered him, "Pursue, for you shall surely overtake them and without fail recover all." So David went, he and the six hundred men who were with him.… And there they were, spread out over all the land, eating and drinking and dancing, because of all the great spoil which they had taken from the land of the Philistines and from the land of Judah. Then David attacked them from twilight until the evening of the next day. Not a man of them escaped, except four hundred young men who rode on camels and fled. So David recovered all that the Amalekites had carried away, and David rescued his two wives. And nothing of theirs was lacking, either small or great, sons or daughters, spoil or anything which they had taken from them; David recovered all. Then David took all the flocks and herds they had driven before those other livestock, and said, "This is David's spoil" (1 Samuel 30:8-9, 16-20).

The Father's desire is that you would go after your inheritance, that you would track it down, that you would overtake everything taken from you, and recover all. That means every blessing and every call that has ever been in your family line all the way back to Adam. That means every mandate that YHVH has ever had and released to your family line that goes all the way back to Adam. It means every ministering angel, every mantle, every throne, every sceptre, every crown, every piece of armour, everything that has ever been mandated for your family and released out of Heaven for your family line that you should have had today, that is now sitting in the spirit. I believe YHVH is saying to us individually and as a global community, "Pursue, overtake, and recover all."

David did some very significant things before he did this; simple little things like he enquired of the Lord, "Shall I go and do this?" Jesus and the Father said to him, "Yes, not only will you overtake and recover, but you will recover all." That means David and his men went in there and everything else that the enemy had taken from every other nation became theirs as well; because an invading army did not just attack David. David just happened to be in their way as they were looting other places. He pursued, overtook and recovered everything.

The Heavens Belong to the Highest Bidder
Many of the ecclesia should be fully manifested as sons in the earth today. The reason some of us are not is because of the capturing of our destiny in the realm of the spirit by demons that know the power of whoever has the highest place causes the fulfilment of their desire, *"So God raised [exalted] him to the highest place"* (Philippians 2:9 EXB), *"God has put Christ over [far above] all rulers, authorities, powers..."* (Ephesians 1:21 EXB). The heavens belong to the highest bidder. Our problem is we are not trading in heaven enough.

We are going to trade on the sea of glass and trade into the Kingdom realm, not only with our finances and our time but also with our desire and with the blood of Jesus; the highest form of trading is blood. That is why devils go after human blood or sacrificial blood, because they know that blood is the highest form of trading. The Bible says that Jesus *"...disarmed the rulers and authorities [those supernatural forces of evil operating against us], He made a public example of them [exhibiting them as captives in His triumphal procession], having triumphed over them through the cross"* (Colossians 2:15 AMP). Jesus has taken the whole of the kingdom that is in darkness, triumphed over it, put them into the arena of His own cart of victory, showing us the power of victory we have. Jesus has already done what is needful for you and me to have total victory over the things around our lives; He has spoiled them. The enemy's motive is to display, to intimidate, to demoralise and to demotivate us and to bring fear into our minds and hearts to make us think that we will be defeated and destroyed. His motive is also to make us fear that if we do anything against the demonic realm that they will come after us and kill us or take us as a spoil themselves. So the church has been standing back, not doing what it is suppose to be doing, because the realm of the Kingdom of God does not manifest around them, as they have not been into the Kingdom. The only way to come into the reality of having everything spoiled around you is to go into Heaven. Father let the whirlwinds of YHVH burn. Hallelujah Father!

The deception that many of us live under is that satan still has dominion; he does not, he only has power where you give him power. The devil has power where you are sinning. There are many believers in ministry today who have fallen and the whole purpose of their life and everything they have had has been taken into a trophy room.

Keys that Unlock the Trophy Room

There are four things that would be helpful for you and your spirit man before even going into some of these arenas:

1. Spending time praying in the spirit – sixteen hours of praying in tongues. If you do that it changes your life. It will change who you are and display what you are to the Kingdom realms. Praying in tongues is vital for your life. The average believer around the world today prays in tongues for two and a half minutes a day. And then we say, "Let us go into warfare," and the devil sees we have not become who we are supposed to be before going there. We have not trained ourselves in the armour that we are supposed to carry in identifying with who we are called to be.

2. Spending time praying and decreeing the Word over your destiny, your generational line and everything that has risen up against your family, that Jesus has spoiled those principalities and powers and made an open show of them totally and absolutely triumphing over them all.

We are so worried about the kingdom that is in darkness that we move our focus from the glory into darkness. Whatever the eye hooks into multiplies. You wonder why you are in such a mess? Shift your focus and come into agreement with what the Word says. We must agree with what the Word says is true. Without it, there is no foundation to stand. Take the Word of God and the potential that is in it and begin to release it around your life.

Do that by praying in tongues first and encountering the Kingdom of God inside you. When you pray the Word of God, you do not just pray it, you **decree** it out of your spirit man, into the spirit world, into an environment around your life, into your body, and command what is there to begin to manifest the Word that you are speaking over it.

Mix it with tongues and also English so you can pray with your understanding as well as with your spirit. An even better way is to pray in the spirit in English so you can understand it while you are praying in the spirit. The Bible says we pray in the languages of men and of angels (1 Corinthians 13:1). Is English a language of men? Yes. It means I can pray in tongues in English. The same way as you speak in tongues, "Father thank You for Your blood and Your glory and Your grace", you do not think about the words that are coming out of your mouth. You let your mouth speak the words the same way as you speak in tongues. It is easy, but we need to practice. "Father, today I thank You that the blood of Jesus Christ cleanses my life."

3. Start to dream about what it is going to be like to be totally liberated and in possession of all your goods. You have got to dream about coming into an inheritance that is powerful, full of dominion, might and glory and full of majesty. Dream about it. Remember, whatever captivates your mind is going to captivate your heart; and whatever captivates your heart is going to come out of your mouth. Have you ever wondered what it is going to be like to be in possession of every single thing that should have been yours from your family line from the glory of the presence of God? You can begin to dream about having back in your possession everything that has been lost to you as the sons of God and the heirs of salvation. Find out what it is going to be like to have the fullness of the glory, of all the glory that YHVH has poured out all the way down your generational line. Oh, I wonder what it is going to be like to have all that back in my possession – everything. Then be able to take that, go into the realm in the Kingdom of God and take that as an offering onto the Sea of Glass and lay it

before the Lord as a covenant offering, praying, "Father, here is my inheritance, Lord trade with it in the Kingdom for nations."

4. Repossess what you have lost; go and get it back. No one else can get it back for you unless YHVH has specifically spoken to them to go and do that. I find there is nothing like practice. You need to practise to get the stuff back that you have lost. You have got to go in there from the glory realm and engage it; get it out, pull it out, become whatever is needed to restore it around your life. You need to dream about it and go in and get hold of it.

In Realms of the Kingdom Volume 1 I have taught about recovering our crowns, which is another specific thing that we need to do as believers. It is the same process and the same defeated demons trying to steal from our lives what belongs to us. They war to strip us of all the dominion that YHVH has given us, so we cannot stand under the government of His Kingdom and then release His government into this arena here. You and I can manifest the Kingdom of God; we have a right to manifest the Kingdom of God and to stand in the realm of the spirit and deal with the demonic arena and shut down their activity. You and I have a mandated authority to actually shut down their cry and their decrees against our lives.

When I went after my inheritance, there were what seemed like four people that looked like me who came into the court. I commanded everything of my DNA in my family line that had ever been procreated or taken into the atmosphere or taken into the realm of the spirit, everything connected to my family line to come into the courtroom. These four things showed up in the courtroom that looked like me because demons know that the higher you go, whatever comes out of Heaven is going to sit in the highest place. So they waylay our destiny and purpose. I went after the whole lot of them and YHVH burnt them in front of me. So I am now the sole heir of everything that comes out of Heaven for me which sits on my life because I now go higher than any demon has ever been, and I trade. Hallelujah Father!

When something has been plundered and spoiled and it has become the possession of another, it is about time you began to plunder his kingdom and take back what belongs to you. It is about time the church got enough grunt to believe that it can take back everything that has been lost to it through Jesus' victory. It is about time the church began to believe that they have a greater Kingdom in them that can destroy another kingdom that has a usurper in it; *"...You are of God and you belong to Him and have [already] overcome them [the agents of the antichrist]; because He who is in you is greater than he (satan) who is in the world..."* (1 John 4:4 AMP); he already knows he is ended. When he shows up and he tries to intimidate you, just show him his future; he is going to burn and he is going to be a nothing. Take him right to the point of that lake and the galaxies beyond what was, at the end of time, where the fire burns and show him, *"The devil, who deceived them, was cast into the lake of fire and... will be tormented day and night forever and ever"* (Revelation 20:10). I can live out of the future; the future is that I win totally, absolutely and positively and the devil is finished. So no matter what happens here, I win, I have this wonderful understanding: I hate him, he hates me and I win! Hallelujah!

Activation
Father, I want to thank You for these people that have listened and tried to get everything that I am saying. Father, what I have shared has been years of my life, the inheritance in an earthen vessel, the treasure in an earthen vessel. Lord I want to give You thanks for my life. Father, thank You that You are enabling Your church and Your body to spoil principalities, because if You have done it, we are going to do it. Then we too will make an open show of triumphing over them in it.

Jesus, I want to thank You for these men and women. I ask for the truth of the reality of what it means to have the treasure restored to them: all that has been lost to them in their generational line. Father, I ask that You would again open the door for these men and women, that in that place they would see Your Kingdom come.

Father, I thank You that this only comes out of ascending into Your presence, that out of Your presence flows the fullness of life. Father, Your cry to pursue, to overtake and to recover all – we receive all from You: all the Kingdom, all the promise, all the purpose, all the destiny, all the dominion, all the power, all the authority, all the holiness, all the righteousness, all the purity, all the sanctification, all the mandate, everything. We receive it from You, Jesus, of the scroll that You have given us to have eternal life on the face of the earth. Jesus, we receive it all from You today. We receive it out of Heaven because we are sons of Heaven. Father, we have the seed of Heaven in us. Lord, we receive all out of Heaven.

Father, we receive all out of Heaven that we too would make an open show of satan, triumphing over him, a triumphant victory, with our inheritance. Father, today I ask that every record of every individual reading this book, of their DNA, where the enemy has ever used that record to waylay the purpose of YHVH, that this record would be brought into court and burnt. Father, today I decree judgement into everything that has been waylaid in the realm of the spirit by another being like them would be burnt in the courts of Heaven, that out of judgment, that justice would come to recover everything, all in the Name of Jesus Christ.

Father I ask that, in the Kingdom, the angels that have been assigned to us would be loosed to do their work, to do the bidding of the Father; every angel that has been assigned to the family, the family line, the city, the church, the tectonic plate, the nation that we live in, that they will be loosed and unleashed to do their work and unleashed to mandate and fight for us on our behalf. Father we receive their ministry today, in the name of Jesus.

Father, I ask that You will bless these people with their treasure in earthen vessels, that You would fill their storehouse to overflowing, pressed down, shaken together and running over, in the Name of Jesus. Hallelujah.

CHAPTER 6

THE FOUR FACES OF GOD

"Four Living Beings, dotted front and back with eyes, stood at the throne's four sides. The first of these Living Beings was in the form of a lion; the second looked like an Ox; the third had the face of a man; and the fourth, the form of an eagle, with wings spread out as though in flight. Each of these Living Beings had six wings, and the central sections of their wings were covered with eyes. Day after day and night after night they kept on saying, "Holy, holy, holy, Lord God Almighty – the one who was, and is, and is to come" (Revelation 4:6-8 TLB).

Engaging with the four faces of God came out of experiences I had that really blew my mind. Each of these faces of God shows us a significant portion of the desire of YHVH to display the facets of His character to us relationally.

My first encounters with the faces of God came out of a period of time when I needed to come into a deeper relationship of intimacy with His presence and get to know Him more. When I want to know someone, I do not just want to be around their presence and smell their fragrance. If my wife walks past and I come in five minutes later, I can smell the perfume that she wears so I know that she was there. Often in a meeting we experience the aroma of YHVH that makes us think, 'Wow!' It is an amazing thing because it draws your heart to Him. But that is not good enough; I do not just want the fragrance of my Father, I want the whole of Him. I want everything there is in relationship with Him. So I set my heart and went after Him. A whole series of things that happened, (see the chapter entitled "The Dark Cloud" in Realms of the Kingdom Volume 1) brought me to an awareness of the dark cloud of God's presence and an understanding of the terror that was associated with that dark cloud around God's presence.

"...The priests could not continue ministering because of the cloud; for the glory of the LORD filled the house of the LORD. Then Solomon spoke: "The LORD said He would dwell in the dark cloud..." (1 Kings 8:11-12). *"So the people stood afar off, but Moses drew near the thick darkness where God was"* (Exodus 20:21). *"When the sun was about to set and a deep sleep fell on Abram, behold, terror of great darkness was falling upon him!"* (Genesis 15:12 TLV).

Finally I came to a point where I stepped through the cloud. It was like a dark cloud with terror, fear, torment, judgment and wrath vibrating on the outside, but the moment I stepped through it there was an absolute peace and tranquillity in the cloud. Then I took another step forward and I was in this little space, like in a circle. God the Father was standing in the rear of the circle. All my religious theories started to tell me that you cannot look at YHVH because you will die so I did not know what to do. But then I realised something that really broke me: there were tears falling on to the floor, and then He said to me, "It's been a long time since anyone has been here, son." I was just lost, it was more than I could handle. But I set my heart to go back again and again because I wanted to spend time with the presence of the person of YHVH.

Looking into God's Face

To me there is nothing more fulfilling than being able to be that close and that real with the person of YHVH. I got over my fear of dying and came to the point where I did not really care if I died because I could not die in any better place. I had all my religious theories telling me that if I see the face of YHVH I will die. Yet in the Bible the Lord says of His servant Moses, *"I speak with him face to face... And he sees the form of the LORD"* (NUMBERS 12:8). The Bible also says, *"The pure in heart... shall see God"* (Matthew 5:8). So I decided to look up into His face, so I lifted my head and looked up into His eyes.

The Bible says, *"The eye is the lamp of the body"* (Matthew 6:22 TLV). Because YHVH is eternal, all of eternity lives inside of Him and as I looked at His eyes I was captivated and drawn towards them and then I started actually being drawn into them. That is where I wanted to be – in Him. It really changed me and gave me a deeper understanding of Jesus' words, *"…As You, Father, are in Me, and I in You; that they also may be one in Us…"* (John 17:21). I am one with the Father because I am actually in Him in eternity. When I was drawn into His eyes, what I saw totally fried my mind, and I know why Enoch did not come back after seeing that – but he wanted to remain there with the person of YHVH, at the deepest point of fellowship we can have. *"Enoch had such a close and intimate relationship with God that one day he just vanished – God took him"* (Genesis 5:24 VOICE). *"By faith [that pleased God] Enoch was caught up and taken to heaven so that he would not have a glimpse of death; AND HE WAS NOT FOUND BECAUSE GOD HAD TAKEN HIM; for even before he was taken [to heaven], he received the testimony [still on record] that he had walked with God and pleased Him"* (Hebrews 11:5 AMP).

Suddenly I withdrew as the grace of YHVH brought me from within the fascination of Him to the knowledge that I did not want to die or to remain there. People needed to know this relationship with Him is possible. I actually began to realize that something was happening with His face so I took a step back. His eyes stayed the same, looking at me totally engaged, with absolute abandoned love. His head was morphing from Lion, to Ox, to Eagle, to Man and back to Lion, over and over. I was blown away, like the angels, in awe, saying, *"Holy, holy, holy"* (Isaiah 6:3). It was really one of the most astounding things I had ever seen in my life because His eyes did not shift, they stayed the same. It was just the whole outside was moving in the sequence of 'YOD–HEY–VAV-HEY'. I did not know about this sequence at that time, but his face was literally morphing just like that. My spirit recognised who He was – He was my Father, not another being or an angel. I began to ponder in my heart, how come no one ever told me this is what I am going to look like? That I am going to have skin like matted diamonds, deep blue, burning with fire, alive and moving, with all the colours of the rainbow mixed. How come no one ever told me I am going to look like that? Because that is what the DNA of God does. We are going to look like that – like Him, the One in whose image we are created.

This encounter gave me a great wonder of the Father. I so valued the time that He gave me to be able to just look at Him like that. The first time I came out of that experience, I came out of the room about an hour and a half later and I was white and shaking, struggling to say anything except "Wow!" My wife asked me what on earth had happened to me because I looked different.

After that I spent weeks, day after day, just living in that sense of the engagement with YHVH for me as a person and as a being, in the knowledge that YHVH actually, truly, really loves me. Every time I went to pray, I would see His face and my whole prayer time would be spent looking at His face feeling, "Whoa! This is what I am going to be like."

I began to have encounters with the different aspects of the person of YHVH. One of my encounters was when I was in Houston. We were praying right in the spirit gateway in Houston Texas, in the area that some of the richest people in the world live. We had started to pray for this area and the people that were there. I had engaged but I was very quiet because something felt really different and I could not figure out what was going on. I heard a movement behind me and I thought somebody was coming towards me. I turned around, and the moment I turned around I was in the spirit. There was a giant Ox that probably would have been about as tall as a two storey building, with a huge neck and head. He had His head up against the pillars of this gate in the spirit and He was pushing at the gate. I felt His cry for the people that were in the Houston area. When He looked at me He made a deep lowing sound that went right through me and into that area. I was on the floor in a mess because I felt the pain of YHVH for those people and the desire of YHVH to see His Kingdom come into them and touch them. The reason I was in such a mess was because I did not know how to comfort the Ox. I did not know what to do with the pain I was feeling of the desperation of YHVH in the Ox, lowing over the lost sheep in that community. Everybody went quiet inside the room. I had lost it because there is nothing you can do to alleviate the pain of the heart of YHVH for people, and His desire for people to get to know Him. I did not know what to do so I just put my arm under the neck of the

Ox and put my head up against Him. I could feel the strain of His heartbeat, and His desire to touch that area. Then I felt Him low again but this time I did not feel the breath, I felt the frequency of His desire, and from His throat, a sound – a deep vibration into my whole body. The cells in my body were aching, responding to His pain.

I can remember feeling all this going on and then coming out of it and everybody asking me what had happened. I told them I just had an encounter with the Ox of YHVH and I did not know what to do. Although I had been doing a bit of study on this, I had not really come to the revelation of it until then. Until you get the revelation of it you can do all the study you like but, once it touches you, it is a totally different thing.

We found out about six months later that there were a whole lot of people in that area who were born again. When the Ox shows up, things happen because of the weight-bearing of His burden.

I have had an encounter with the Lion of God; He showed up in a similar kind of way. He came up to me and He put His face up against me and He breathed into my chest. Again everything changes when you have this kind of encounter with YHVH. I wanted to teach on the four faces of God because each of them symbolise a very specific characteristic of our Father.

YHVH has chosen to reveal Himself and the nature of who He is, within our four-dimensional arena, in these ways. These manifestations of Himself can encapsulate His desire for relationship with us, His sons, so He has chosen to carry these four faces. The living creatures that are around YHVH also have four faces. The reason they have four faces is that they have spent eternity in His presence, and they have taken on His image because we are changed into the likeness of whatever we look upon. *"And we all, with unveiled face, continually seeing as in a mirror the glory of the Lord, are progressively being transformed into His image from [one degree of] glory to [even more] glory, which comes from the Lord, [who is] the Spirit"* (2 Corinthians 3:18 AMP). They have spent eternity looking at the person, the faces and the glory of God, and they have taken on the image and reflection of the One they worship.

I went through this process of looking at these different

creatures and trying to wrestle with my feelings. There were times when the Ox would be present as I was lying down. He would put His chin on my chest and the weight of the glory would come over my life. The point is that we do not need to do anything. All YHVH wants to do is just to hang out with us for a little while, for us to take a little bit of His weight and some of His feelings and bear them with Him. That is what families do and YHVH wants to bear those things with us.

I began to recognise that there were important characteristics that we need to get to grips with in regard to the person of YHVH.

The Ox

The Ox is the burden bearer that carries the responsibility for the shepherding of the sheep.

He symbolises strength and endurance. The Lord talks about breaking the yoke throughout the Bible.

"Is this not the fast that I have chosen:
To loose the bonds of wickedness,
To undo the heavy burdens,
To let the oppressed go free" (Isaiah 58:6)

"Take My yoke upon you and learn from Me, for I am gentle and lowly in heart, and you will find rest for your souls" (Matthew 11:29).

"...Why do you test God by putting a yoke on the neck of the disciples which neither our fathers nor we were able to bear?" (Acts 15:10).

The ox is a burden bearer. Through endurance, obedience is obtained. Patience is one of the attributes of an ox. An ox is very patient in the way it does things, and because it is so big it just does not care about the opinions of other things around it. It is so big it will just go where it wants to, do what it wants, at the pace it wants and it will get the job done. That is the way oxen are. It is an amazing creature, and the Ox of God is an amazing being. When the Bible tells us to heal the sick in Jesus' Name (Matthew 10:8), that is the Ox of God roaring. The Seven Spirits of God are also entwined with these four faces (Isaiah 11:2), and the Ox is directly linked to the Spirit of Might.

You and I need to yoke ourselves to the Ox of God, so that YHVH can move through our lives to bring us to a point where we are totally obedient through his obedience to the Father. Jesus is the chief Ox and my chief Rabbi, and so I yoke myself to Him so that He can bring me through my trials, never having to walk through them by myself. One thing about yoking yourself to the Ox of God is that you will never ever be alone. When you find it difficult, He will carry you through because of the shared yoke. I fell in love with the Ox of God when I had that encounter in Dallas.

This face our Father chooses to reveal to us symbolises a number of things, the most obvious being strength and endurance. An ox is a burden bearer. This creature is very patient and very obedient. The ox is an amazing animal. In Israel's day, when they wanted to train a young ox to plough a field or when they wanted it to do something, they would take a big ox that weighed about 2500 lbs and put a yoke around the big ox with a smaller yoke connected to it by a plank. They would then lock a young ox into that yoke and put the plough behind the big ox. The big ox would walk around the field because the big ox knew the job. It knew what to do and it would go and do the job. The young ox would get frustrated and irritable. It would kick its heels, struggle to get free and go off to do what it wanted to do. It would get to a stage where the young ox would get so furious about wanting to go and do what it wanted to do that they would get something called a goad, which was a plank with little barbs sticking out of it. This would be hung behind the young ox's back legs. So when the young ox got furious and kicked its back legs to try to kick the person, it would kick these things, which would hurt. So eventually it learnt not to kick and struggle.

It is amazing how much we are like this young ox when we are so busy and wanting to do our own thing and yet YHVH has a plan and a purpose. We can kick and scream but we are each yoked to Him. Sometimes a young ox will refuse to move and just sit on the ground, so the big 2500 lb ox will just drag it along. Who is going to win, the 500 lb ox or the 2500 lb ox? That is how they train the ox to do the job, or to be the weight bearer, the burden bearer, the one that ploughs and the one that does the work. It is like us and one of the important things I learnt out of this is that I needed to yoke myself to the presence of God, willingly and freely out of my own will and choice; being willing to yoke myself to Him, no matter how badly my desires or feelings wanted to go and do my own thing. YHVH yoked me to Himself and He would pull me along until I learnt His ways, so I chose to walk with Him freely. I have tried putting a yoke around my neck so that I could get a feeling of what it was like to be yoked to the presence of God. Then I began to pray, "Father thank You that I have yoked myself to You willingly and freely. I give You permission to drag me through anything you need to drag me through to make me able to do the work that You want me to do and do the things that You do; I yoke myself to You today."

There were times when I did not want to do what YHVH wanted me to do. There are times when it is really hard to go and do the things you do not want to do, and the things you want to do you cannot do because you are yoked to something else. But I found that YHVH is so faithful when we turn to Him. He says, *"Come to Me, all you who labor and are heavy laden, and I will give you rest. Take My yoke upon you and learn from Me, for I am gentle and lowly in heart, and you will find rest for your souls"* (Matthew 11:28-29). I found that if I put myself as close as I can to the Ox of God – to the person of YHVH in that form, He carries all the things I struggle with in my life, because He is the one that bears the big yoke. Then His yoke for me, which comes from Him around my life, is easy, and my burden is light.

I found that by spending the time being close to Him like that, many of the issues that I should have gone through, and struggled with, were not a struggle, and I have been able to walk through them because I have been yoked to the presence of God.

The Eagle
Another one of the faces of my Father is an eagle and He is amazing. Nature only reflects a small portion of the supernatural reality of what and who He is. The Eagle is symbolised by the Sprit of Wisdom and the Spirit of Knowledge.

The eagle is free and uninhibited. One of the greatest, most liberating experiences I had in my own personal life was when I realised that YHVH was free and uninhibited, totally abandoned to life and absolutely given over to enjoying life.

The eagle is very symbolic of liberty and majesty. The eagle is the hunter, a trainer and the one that can see into the future. An eagle is an absolutely patient nest builder and the eagle of God is all about personal encouragement. I have done a lot of study on eagles because I wanted to understand them. There are some amazing books I found including Jamie Buckingham's "Where Eagles Soar". I went into the library and borrowed every book on eagles I could find and studied diagrams describing eagles.

There are some amazing things we know about eagles. When an eagle gets to a certain height it will lock its wings using a certain joint and its wings will never bend from that point. This enables it to do what we know as soaring, carried up by the currents of wind.

Pilots have recorded sightings of eagles as high as 10,000ft up in the air. Their respiratory system and heart rate can slow right down when it is soaring. Amazingly an eagle can see a rat on the face of the earth from a very high altitude. It can also see another bird flying in the air and it will watch it from a great height until it is ready to make a move.

When we were children we used to live near a place in South Africa called Kloof, near Durban. There was a big gorge there with a river that ran through it and there were two black king eagles that used to live in the gorge. We did not have TV so we used play outside a lot and we would hear the eagles early in the morning. They would cry and we would go outside, lie on our backs and see how long we could keep our eyes on the eagle until we lost sight of it. What we really loved was listening for the crying to stop because we knew that within about thirty seconds one of us would spot this black thing swooping down out of the sky at a massive speed. It was just the most amazing sight to see.

At the right time YHVH will come in and interfere in your life circumstances and completely change them. His eye has never ever left any one of us. No matter how far away He seems to be, His eye is always upon each of us, always watching over you and me, always desiring the best for us.

When an eagle nests, the female puts her nest in the cleft of a rock next to a sheer drop. The reason she does this is that she wants to teach her chicks how to fly when the time is right. She builds her nest out of thorns, with rocks and stones underneath, that stick out like barbs into the nest. She then fills up the nest with lovely soft fluffy down. She lays the eggs on the fluffy down and other fluffy pelts she finds to make it nice and warm and cosy. Then the eaglets sit inside the nest nice and comfortable in a lovely position. But then the mother eagle gets to a stage where the babies need to leave the nest because their feathers have grown. The mother eagle gets bored with having the babies in the nest, so she begins to take the down out of the nest. She pulls it out so the eaglets are left sitting on thorns and stones. So the most comfortable place for them to sit is on the edge of the nest. They will sit there and wait for her to come. After some weeks when she gets bored of them sitting on the edge of the nest and not doing anything, she will get behind one of them and use her beak to knock it out of the nest. The young eagle will be falling down, upside down, waving its wings around trying to fly. Now the mother will swoop down underneath the baby, pick it up, take it right out over a cliff somewhere high up upon the air currents and drop it again. She will then swoop down with it, and again pick the baby up on her wings and take it back to the nest. She will then start with the next one. She teaches her chicks how to fly in this way.

The Lord says in the Word:

"...I bore you on eagles' wings and brought you to Myself" (Exodus 19:4)
"...He encircled him, He instructed him,
He kept him as the apple of His eye.
As an eagle stirs up its nest,
Hovers over its young,
Spreading out its wings, taking them up,
Carrying them on its wings..."
So the LORD alone led him" (Deuteronomy 32:10-12).

"But those who wait for the LORD [who expect, look for, and hope in Him] Will gain new strength and renew their power; They will lift up their wings [and rise up close to God] like eagles [rising toward the sun]" (Isaiah 40:31 AMP).

When you are learning how to fly, your Father comes as an eagle and picks you up and teaches you how to learn to function in the world of His kingdom.

One thing I know about YHVH is that if you want to engage Him and you are serious about it, He will make the nest very uncomfortable. So what you find is that YHVH makes the religious status quo become very uncomfortable and you find yourself sitting on the edge of the nest. The unfortunate part about it is that many people who get knocked out of the nest fall away, because they are so immature, all they want is to be fed by mother eagle. They do not want to go and feed themselves or come into revelation for themselves, they just want to be fed by someone else.

The Golden Eagle can live for decades and at a certain age it will find a cave in the side of a cliff somewhere where no animals can access it and strip every single feather from its body. It will then beat its beak up against a rock until it starts to bruise around the edge of the beak and then the beak falls off. It has an oil sack that sits on its back and it squashes that oil sack with its soft pliable mouth and begins to massage the oil all over its skin. The oil stimulates new growth, which is the same as what Holy Spirit does. He comes to us as oil to stimulate new growth. So if you are going through a season of stripping the reason is that there is something better coming.

The eagle then massages the oil into its body every day and new feathers begin to form on its body. It gets renewed, like being reborn. It is a completely new eagle when it is finished, with a new beak, new claws, and new feathers. This is what the Holy Spirit wants to do with us. He wants to create in us a new being so that we come out with a new beak, new claws and new feathers as a new being.

I had an encounter with the Eagle of God when I was in the spirit just about to go through the snake line[3]. I heard a squealing sound like – "tzzzzzh, tzzzzzh". It was the cry of the Eagle saying, "Come and fly with Me." Again, I had the most amazing experience with the presence of YHVH, both of us moving as winged beings. All these things solidify in me the depth of desire to go on and on and chase Him until I get to the point of being like Him.

The Man

The face of the Man is connected with emotions and feelings, He is empathetic. The Man face of God symbolises vulnerability where His feelings can be seen and related to. It enables Him to be able to touch our hearts and allows us to be able to touch Him. The Man is expressive and vulnerable. He has the ability to feel and experience those kinds of things with us. It enables Him to not only relate by touch, but also to be able to express emotions. Do you realise that YHVH expresses emotions?

"Leave Me alone so that My anger can flare up and destroy them"
(Exodus 32:10 VOICE).
"He will rejoice over you with gladness, He will quiet you with His love, He will rejoice over you with singing" (Zephaniah 3:17).
"He who sits in heaven laughs!" (Psalm 2:4 TLV).
"Jesus wept" (John 11:35).
"I will rejoice in Jerusalem, And joy in My people" (Isaiah 65:19).
"These things I have spoken to you, that My joy may remain in you"
(John 15:11).
"Behold, he comes Leaping upon the mountains, Skipping upon the hills…" (Song of Solomon 2:8).

By the way, it is fun, you should try doing it sometime – thought speed transport from mountain top to mountain top – 'Catch me if you can' around and around the earth.

These things all build relational connection. The Man aspect of the Father empowers us to build relational connection with Him.

---

[3] Editor's note: Ian refers to the snake line as the point in the spirit realm past which the demonic cannot go and above which is only holiness and the grace of God's blessing.

That is all He wants: relational connection. You know what your life is like and how vulnerable it is. When the face of God is like a man He is very vulnerable, that is why, in the garden, I have never seen the face of God as an Eagle, an Ox or a Lion. He always has the form of a man. When I was in the dark cloud He was always a man because that is the vulnerable part, where the Father is saying, "I want to be vulnerable to you as my child, and I want you to be able to touch Me and speak with Me".

Everything about the Father is about relationship and His desire to come into that whole arena of relationship. The Man is symbolised by the Spirit of Understanding and Counsel. The other thing about the Man is that He is also uninhibited. There is an abandoned freedom to love and be loved inside the face of the Man.

God in the form of a Man empowers us to be around our Father and actually relate to Him as a Man. You walk side by side with a man not face-to-face. With a girl you meet face to face, with a man you move side by side – relationship stuff. And so the first time I saw the Father in Eden by the rose garden, I went and stood beside Him while He pruned roses. They are the most amazing things because they are alive when He prunes them, and the cuttings fall but, because nothing dies, it goes into the ground and becomes life and a new rosebud shoots forth. Standing side by side is an example of the things we can walk through with the presence of God.

When the Bible says, *"As you go, preach, saying, 'The kingdom of heaven is at hand.' Heal the sick..."* (Matthew 10:7-8), that is the Man of God manifesting.

The Lion

The Lion is the fierce protector. The lion symbolises the King. It is about ruler-ship and about the establishing of boundaries. It sets in place Lordship. It releases authority and dominion and the fear of the presence of another that is stronger.

When the Bible says, *"In My name they will cast out demons..."* (Mark 16:17), that is the Lion roaring.

The Lion is directly linked to the Spirit of the Fear of the Lord, and the Spirit of the Lord. The Lion establishes boundaries and brings kingship, ruler-ship, Lordship, authority, dominion, and power.

I have done studies on the natural arenas associated with each animal. The lion is an amazing creature in the things it does in the wild, in the way it hunts and how it sets up and looks after its pride. A male lion cares for his female lions in certain ways. He looks after them in the way he hunts and the expressive things he does with his mouth when he roars. He will get on top of a hill at night time in the cool of the day and he will roar into the atmosphere to establish the arena of his dominion. YHVH roars over us to establish to the whole spiritual world that He has got dominion here over this temple. The Father is like a lion to us individually because He roars over each of us. He speaks into us and breathes into us; He gives us the ability to become the fierce one and the hunter.

I love hunting out and killing demons and because of the lion nature that YHVH has given us, we have the capacity to do these things. When things come around your life, engage each of these natures that YHVH wants us to know.

One of the things I have found with YHVH is that He wants to protect us. His desire is to overshadow each of us, to cover us and to roar over us in protection. If we come into relationship with Him we are going to look like Him, and we are going to be like Him, which means that He is going to enable us to roar over others, to overshadow others, to protect them and to do the same things He does. This is not only over others but over a city, then over nations, then over continental plates, then over the earth, then over the judgment seats, then over the ruler-ship seats and then over the different mountains that go up into the mountain of the Lord (Psalm 24:3, Isaiah 2:2).

Some time ago I was in the spirit over our city and holding our city in my heart and trying to figure out what I needed to do to deal with some of the things in my territory and in my nation, and on our tectonic plate. Again, I felt this movement behind me very similar to what I had felt before, except now I felt a fear. My immediate reaction was that a demon spirit had shown up –

because I could feel fear. So it took me a few minutes to identify that fear. When I identified that fear it was not the fear of being afraid of a demonic spirit, it was the fear of being in the presence of absolute power. So then I was really terrified because I wondered what on earth was standing behind me as I felt that feeling, and when I turned around there was a Lion looking at me. He looked at me while He opened His mouth and roared into me. I fell on the floor. I felt like running away because I wanted to get away from the sound of the roar that was coming into the sound of my body. I was saying inside, "God, I can't handle this anymore!" But it did not stop; the roar continued. I realised God was roaring into me the sound of government. I wondered, "Why hasn't anybody told me that this is what our God is like?"

I was in church a number of months later, in the meeting at the back of the church, and I heard the sound of the roar again. I turned around and there was the Lion, and He roared into me and right through me again. I was on the floor sobbing and shaking.

These encounters with the presence of the Lord in that dimensional way have really given me an understanding of the power of His name – so that when you are on the outside of it, receiving it, it is unbelievably cool but terrifyingly amazing, wonderful, awesome, draining and fearsome all at once. I do not know how you describe these emotions. It is like everything you have ever experienced put into a little box and blended altogether.

The more you yield yourself to the presence of God and come into relationship with Him, the greater your experience will be of His kingdom in your life.

These four aspects of God are very important to us as individuals. They empower us to be able to understand not only what we are going to look like, but actually how to display and bear His image properly. Unless you engage and understand the process with these four sides of God's nature, you will not be able to display these aspects of His character properly. When you understand and engage these four sides of His nature it destroys the yoke of belief systems cultured by your parents around your life. It shatters all the rejection, the isolation, the loneliness, the pessimism, the unbelief, the shock, the trauma, the rejection, the self rejection, the fear of rejection and the shame. It shatters absolutely every demonic spirit, because they cannot stand in the face of God.

YHVH said to Abraham, *"When Abram was 99 years old, ADONAI appeared to Abram, and He said to him, "I am El Shaddai. Continually walk before Me and you will be blameless"* (Genesis 17:1 TLV). In the original Hebrew language it says, "Turn towards My faces, walk towards them, and I will make you flawless." That is because everything is about the faces of God – everything. Dealing with your humanity is about the faces of God. That is why we have got to position ourselves in His Name, because in His Name, and I do not mean casually like a lucky charm, but actually in His Name every devil will flee because they cannot stand the provision of those four faces. In His Name, every knee shall bow. Why? Because of the power that is displayed in the love that is in those four faces. In His Name, you will heal the sick, you will bind up the broken hearted. Why? Because there is complete restoration available in the four faces of God, because of the way that they can become empathic with us as human beings. Is God four beings? No, He is one, but he has four ways of expression at all times.

I found understanding His nature really helped me to have relationship with YHVH. The Bible says, *"...God is love"* (1 John 4:8). We read that but actually our experience of Him being love is not yet real for most of us. If YHVH is love, then we have got to understand that those four faces will release around us so much love, and that love commands a response. Love is not an emotion, love is a choice and an act of your will. Did you realise that? You have got to choose to love. That is why the Bible says, *"Beloved, let us love one another, for love is of God; and everyone who loves is born of God and knows God. He who does not love does not know God..."* (1 John 4:7-8).

These things about the nature and character of YHVH are so important for us because they reveal His nature to us and so we are empowered to become relational beings with the God of the universe. When I go into the realm of the presence of God, I do not go running up to the throne of God when He is in His full dominion and power and say, "Daddy, can I have a hug? Can I say hello to you today?" You can when you are three years old and still sucking your thumb. But when you are aged 25 and you say,

"Dad, can I have a hug?" No one will say how cute you are because maturity requires us to carry responsibility.

I have found that it is best not to go and approach my Father when He is on His throne in all His power and all the dominion of ruler-ship, where He wears the garment of a King and has the sceptre of the government of Heaven in his hand. Otherwise I would get fried to a crisp! We have got to learn protocol. When the Father comes off the seat of His government, that is when you learn how to relate to Him. The governmental seat gives us the understanding that He is the God of the universe, full of power and might and authority, dominion and glory. But even though He has all of that, we can still touch Him as a Father. We can still be around Him and, not only does He want us to be around Him, He wants us to learn how to sit beside Him so we can learn to carry and bear His image into all of creation.

The Bible says, *"And as we have borne the image of the man of dust, we shall also bear the image of the heavenly Man" (1 Corinthians 15:49).* That is the statement I have been looking for all my life. After I had done studies on all these things, I do not know how many times I have read that verse. I do not know how many times I have read the Bible through and through but, when the Lord gave me this scripture, it absolutely blew my mind. I was looking at Him and asking Him why no one ever told me I was going to look like that. He is now saying to you and me, 'You are going to be like that'. That makes me very excited. I am looking forward to walking down the street with beams of light shining out of me, and my head morphing between the Lion, the Ox, the Eagle, and the Man!

Activation
Father, I want to thank You for who You are. Father, I want to thank You that You have made us uniquely designed to bear Your image. Father, according to the Word, You said that as we have born the image of the earthly, so we shall bear the image of the heavenly.

Father, today I bless these people with the knowledge of what they will bear out of the heavenly arena. Father, I bless them with the knowledge that we are able to attain to these things. That it is not based on our faith but it is based on what Jesus' faith has already done and accomplished for us.

Lord, today we hook into that law of faith. Father, we hook into that law of faith, because out of that faith we are going to bear the image of the most high God, born out of His seed, becoming like Him, in Jesus' Name. Amen.

CHAPTER 7

THE FOUR CHAMBERS OF THE HEART

The four chambers of the heart are: the garden of the heart, the dance floor, the soaking room of preparation and the bridal chamber. I would like to teach on these subjects from my own personal experience.

First Chamber – Personal Garden

The first chamber of the heart is the personal garden. When the Lord began to speak to me about the four chambers of the heart, I spent two and a half years cultivating the garden of my heart, so that the presence of God could come out of the realm of Eden and walk into my garden and I could have fellowship with Him in my garden as well as in His garden.

"And they heard the sound of the LORD God walking in the garden in the cool [afternoon breeze] of the day..." (Genesis 3:8 AMP).

"Awake, O north wind,
And come, south wind [blow softly upon my garden];
Make my garden breathe out fragrance, [for the one in whom my soul delights],
Let its spices flow forth.
Let my beloved come into his garden and eat its choicest fruits" (Song of Solomon 4:16 AMP).

When I used to go through things with the Lord, I wanted a living record of the testimony, so I learned to plant a seed of each victory in my garden praying, "Father this is a seed that will grow into a cedar of Lebanon inside my garden as a testimony to what we have done together here today."

The first time I ever planted something, my heart was a desert. Unless we have cultivated our gardens, they are deserts. So I planted a seed, and when I turned around there was a tree. Remember that light and power equals mass: $E = mc^2$. Out of the desire of YHVH, things are created. RNA can be described as "revealed nature achieved". Out of the RNA of the testimony of YHVH, He creates things – YHVH is into creating. I grew my garden and did all these wonderful things, so I have a lovely garden where I go and spend time with the Father. Of course, my garden gives me access to His garden, so I can go and walk in Eden (see chapter entitled 'Eden' in Realms of the Kingdom Volume 1). We will look at the process of cultivating the personal garden of the heart more deeply in the next chapter.

Second Chamber – The Dance Floor

The other three chambers of the heart are also very important. I went through the process of getting an understanding of them. The first chamber of the heart is a garden. The second chamber of the heart is the dance floor, since everything to do with YHVH and the river of God always stems out of intimacy. When the Lord began to speak to me about dancing with His presence, springing along the mountaintops, engaging His presence, whirling in the glory, dancing among the candlesticks of the presence of God, all these things were exhilarating to me. I got lost in the love experience and euphoria of YHVH's desire for me to just be with Him. YHVH wants each of us to be with Him even more than you and I want Him to be with us.

This is why YHVH called to Adam in the garden, "*Where are you?*" (Gen 3:9 NKJV). It was not just because Adam had sinned, but it was the loss of relationship, friendship and intimacy. When I was in the dark cloud and the Lord was weeping, He said that it had been a long time since anyone had been there and I was undone (see chapter entitled 'The Dark Cloud' in Realms of the Kingdom Volume 1). So, this realm of the dance floor became a very important thing for me.

I did not know what to do – I am male; I think like a man. But when YHVH told me to wear an earring[4] I had to forget that and be obedient because I am a bondservant. I do not have to wear it anymore, because I am a son, but I choose to wear it to challenge the religious spirit.

I began to think about this dance floor and what it would be like. I thought about some of the places I have been to in the realm of the Kingdom and some of the experiences I had encountered. I realized that this had actually been different from the way I imaged it would be.

In one of my first encounters as I was beginning to love on YHVH, I was just worshipping in the Spirit, beginning to engage and the atmosphere got heavier and heavier. My spirit man began to engage the presence of YHVH and seemed to came out of me and melt into Him. As that transference happened, I found myself walking into a massively big hallway with great big pillars. I could not see the top because it was all smoke, mist and clouds. I knew I was in the spirit when I walked onto the floor, and I was barefoot yet my feet made the sounds of stilettos on marble, 'click, click, click, click'. I did not know what to do, but because I had been engaging the presence of God I thought, 'Well Lord, I can do nothing better than to go back to where I was'. So I started to engage and began to worship again. When you are in the Kingdom and start to worship, your words echo into the spirit Kingdom world, and I heard them beginning to bounce from wall to wall. The first word never stops bouncing, it just carries on and then you add more to it and it starts to make a cacophonous sound. Then gradually a canopy is built and the whole angelic world turns up because a son is singing to the Father, and they respond, "Let's go join in!" Heaven's desire, as YHVH's desire is to sing over us with joy. *"The LORD your God in your midst, The Mighty One, will save; He will rejoice over you with gladness, He will quiet you with His love, He will rejoice over you with singing"* (Zephaniah 3:17 NKJV).

---

[4] *"But if the servant shall plainly say, I love my master, my wife, and my children; I will not go free, Then his master shall bring him to God [the judges as His agents]; he shall bring him to the door or doorpost and shall pierce his ear with an awl; and he shall serve him for life"* (Exodus 21:5-6 AMP).

So I was in this room with a lot of chaotic atmospheric intensity going on, and I thought, 'So I am just going to...? I mean, I am a guy who is going to what – boogie-woogie?' I did not know what to do. I just said in my spirit man that I would start to move my body and by faith I began to give myself in an expressive way to the presence of God – to dance before His presence.

I was not expecting Him to come and engage me and dance with me. I am a man, how do you dance with another man? That is how we think when we are in the flesh. But as a spirit being there is neither male nor female (Galatians 3:28). It is union, spirit to spirit. I began to give my spirit man to the presence of God, to actually begin to move with His glory and anointing inside that room.

There was a lot of noise, and I got lost. I got totally and absolutely lost in what was going on in this interaction for maybe an hour. I had no reference for time, because when we are in the Kingdom, time just does not exist in the same way. We are out of time and space there, and what can be five minutes here can be five hours there and what can be five hours there can be three seconds here. There is no common frame of reference for time. I danced with the presence of God and then began to become aware that there were other people inside the room on the dance floor. At first I had my eyes closed. I do not know why I had my eyes closed except that I had given myself over and shut everything else out to focus on what was happening in my relationship with the presence of the Father.

I realized that there were others inside the dance floor and my mind started saying, 'Oh my gosh, I wonder what they are going to think about me when they know that I have danced here with YHVH. I am dancing with YHVH, wow...!' While I was going through all these thoughts, I opened my eyes to see who they were and when I did, I found the embrace of the Godhead around me. I had the Father, Son and Holy Spirit dancing a pirouette around me on the dance floor. Now I really started to fall in love and get lost. I did not care what anyone thought because I was in the best place I could ever be.

On the outside of me, a whirlwind began to form. I know what whirlwinds do because I have been on them in the spirit and have traveled on them to galaxies. So when this whirlwind began to form around me I started to wonder where YHVH was taking me, but nothing happened. When I opened my eyes again, a reverse tornado had formed over the top of me, with a big base at the bottom that went to a fine point up in the mist somewhere. I found myself outside of this canopy watching my body start to dissolve. It was kind of falling to bits, dissolving into this mist that was the Father, Son and Holy Spirit inside this swirling cloud. I was dissolving into nothing and watching this, and I was amazed. It is amazing what we can do in the Kingdom world.

I saw myself dissolve and I was in the mist again, still me, fully aware of every single particle of what I was, still correlated together yet it was all separate, because it was in total unity with the Father. I went up into this mist, and as I got higher and higher up I could see a light at the top of the tunnel I was in. The closer I got to it, the more reality I began to see. It was not actually a hole, but a three stranded cord of DNA that was in the top of this tunnel. I found myself going up into the top of the tunnel and swirling around the DNA. I knew what was going on and what was going to happen, because I had been studying it all.

Suddenly there was a "click"; the DNA strand had disappeared but I could feel it in me. It was in the fibre of the record of what I had been pushing to engage for many years – it was now in my being. I came down out of the cloud and I watched myself reform into Ian, but I was different. Something had gone on inside of me that had brought me into an accord with the Father's testimony and His record in Heaven. We all need to have encounters with the records of the testimonies that YHVH designed for us to walk in before we were on the earth, not just the testimonies of our parent's records that we now walk in. *"For we are His workmanship, created in Christ Jesus for good works, which God prepared beforehand that we should walk in them"* (Ephesians 2:10 NKJV).

Jesus gave us the record and the testimony of His Body and blood which carries the DNA of our Heavenly Father in communion. (See the chapter entitled the DNA of God in Realms of the Kingdom Volume 1).

I had come back down out of the cloud and was reformed, but I was still lost in the experience of it all, and I was also trying to look inside myself to figure out what had happened. Then I found myself back on the earth in my room, still worshipping in the spirit. We have to learn our spirit pathways in and out. We should never just close our spiritual experiences abruptly and walk away. We have to learn how to back out. We should never turn our backs on the presence of God, but back away slowly and sensitively, so we can remember the way back in.

Third Chamber – The Soaking Room of Preparation

The third chamber of the heart is known as the soaking room of preparation. This room is described well in the book of Esther. When Queen Esther was being prepared to become the bride of the king, she spent a year soaking in spices and incense that purified her body (Esther 2:12). With my experiences of the garden and the dance floor, I have learned that everything is about intimacy.

I always find that worship is a key that can unlock the boundaries set around me, to bring me through desire and intimacy, into an encounter with YHVH, which takes me into deeper levels of relationship. I am not chasing the experience. I just want YHVH, but I am aware of a platform that can form a stepping stone to engage a deeper relationship with YHVH, so I will hold to that platform, but I do not look to the platform to be my experience, it is just a platform. The Soaking Room of the preparation of the bride for the bridegroom is another platform. I began to engage the presence of God while holding the platform of the knowledge of what YHVH needed me to do here, and I began to turn my heart towards Him there, to purposefully engage out of my desire to know Him.

I do not stay in this physical realm and engage from here to experience revelation of Him. I go into His presence to engage Him to bring revelation back into this realm. This is a major issue because our tendency is to be here and try to engage from here, thinking that we want the spiritual experiences which will unify us with YHVH, but we have to engage YHVH first with the understanding that the experiences will come out of our engagement with YHVH.

I began to engage this platform, knowing that it has to do with herbs, spices, incense, frequencies, and all the wave patterns of the whole of the realm of Heaven. I also knew that it has to do with the whole realm of worship and abandonment, the expression of the sound of my DNA, the expression of the frequency of what I carry, the electromagnetic energy that flows from cell to cell in my body, with light, the colors of light and what it means to live in the light. It has to do with all these things because they are really all one in the Kingdom.

While engaging the realm of intimacy I began to look towards the presence of the Lord with this platform in mind praying, "Father, I need You to bring revelation of this, but Lord, even if You do not do that I am just going to love You. I am going to purposefully chase You until You get so sick of me chasing You that You are going to show me what this is all about." We have to do these kind of things – I set my heart to engage the presence of the Lord like this.

Again, I found myself at a doorway – there are four doors of the heart which need to be open. With any door, the function is for us to open it and go through. Many of us stand at the door but do not go in because we are afraid of what is going to happen when we go in. But mostly we are afraid that these encounters with YHVH will make us have to deal with our junk.

I opened the door and went into fire, mist, sound, color and fragrance – it was like walking into a warm bath. "*...Christ loved the church and gave himself for her to make her holy [sanctify her], cleansing her in the washing of water by the word*" (Ephesians 5:25-26 EXB). I walked into it and thought, 'Oh this is amazing' and I just fell into it. How long I stayed there I do not know. This is where the love kisses of YHVH come in, "*Let him kiss me with the kisses of his mouth – For your love is better than wine*" (Song of Solomon 1:2 NKJV). He goes into the very fibre of our beings and prepares tables in us for the Father to come and meet with us in our DNA Psalm 23:5. He soaks the records of who we are in the testimony of what He is to change the sounds and fragrances of who we are, as the Bible says, "*We are the sweet fragrance of Christ...unto God...among those who are being saved and among those who are perishing*" (2 Corinthians 2:15 AMP).

I began to have this encounter of soaking in this lightning, fire, vibrating sound, awesome smelling, wonderful, amazing experience. I was there for hours. I would drag myself out, go to work, come home, find that nobody was home, go back into the room and spend the whole night time in the Soaking Room. Then I would drag myself out again, go to work, come home to, "Hi honey, how are you going? Glad to see you today; you are wonderful." Then at around half past nine or ten o'clock I would say, "See you, I am going to bed". I would go into my room and *whoosh*. I spent weeks soaking in the preparation bath of the glory of God to prepare me as a son in union with Him.

Fourth Chamber – The Bridal Chamber

The last chamber of the heart is the bridal chamber. This is where we are joined and become one with the presence of God. The Bible says, "The person who is united to the Lord becomes one spirit with Him" (1 Corinthians 6:17 AMP).

The bridal chamber has nothing to do with sexual union. There are some weird people who twist what I say and come out with accusations of that nature. It is a deception to try to take something that is on earth and put it into Heaven. The Bible says, "...On earth as it is in heaven" (Matthew 6:10 NKJV), not in Heaven as it is on earth. We must not take an earthly thing that keeps you tied in chaos and try to put it into Heaven. But instead we need to take authority over earthly things using Heaven's memories and Heaven's engagement to bring them into alignment as it is in Heaven.

In the natural world we have sexual union between a husband and wife where their spirits are knit together. Our Father designed sex for marriage because of the established Biblical covenant that happens between a man and a woman. What they do not talk about in the media, in school presentations, or in any of the things that are taught today is what happens spiritually when a man releases his seed into a woman's body.

They used to think that the seed would be washed away. What they realized after doing tests was that the woman actually assimilates the seed into her body and her body begins to take on the sound of the man through the DNA.

So people who go sleeping around, end up with the sound of however many different partners inside their bodies. When they go on to get married and a woman then tries to have unity with her husband, she has the sound of many other men embedded inside her body; and the same thing happens with men when they have united with lots of different women.

Not only does transference happen, but if people have sexual partners who are involved in the occult, they create soul ties that keep them connected to each other and those people involved in the occult can then draw on the lives of the people that they are soul tied to, for their own personal benefit. When they are feeling down for example, they can engage the hook of the sound that is in the people they are soul-tied to, and pull on them, drawing energy from those people's bodies and lives.

Then there is the fact that demons can be connected with the seed. When the seed gets released, there can be a spirit attached, particularly when attitudes are based in lust. When the seed gets transferred, the demon gets hold of that body and that person may then struggle with the spirit of lust.

This does not often get taught or talked about, but it literally fractures lives. We wonder why we cannot get engaged properly and have good godly marriages, then come to find out it is because we are soul-tied and connected in sound frequencies inside our DNA with demons and other people around the face of the earth.

I hate what the enemy is doing amongst our young people with the promiscuity and the spirit that is behind that thing trying to destroy people. It is not okay to sleep around. The Bible says, *"... Do not be misled. A lot of people stand to inherit nothing of God's coming kingdom, including those whose lives are defined by sexual immorality..."* (1 Cor 6:9-10 VOICE). We say that we want signs and wonders. Well I am sorry it is not going to happen through people who are doing this.

We think this is okay because the media presents it to us from Hollywood, which very often acts as a doorway of Hell but should be a doorway to the Kingdom, and needs to change. We think that it is okay because we get so blinded and bombarded by information that forms a platform in the frequency and in the water in our bodies, carrying the message that tells us it is all okay, that it does not really matter and that it is okay to have homosexual relationships and that no one really knows because it is all done in secret. But actually, we are never alone.

YHVH made Adam and Eve. I do not care what the school books are teaching, or what propaganda is getting put into the preschools today. YHVH made them male and female; everything else is outside the boundaries of the presence of God and will not inherit the Kingdom. The reason I am saying this is because some believers are involved in this and they need to deal with it. I know this because I can see it.

The bridal chamber is very important for us with regard to our unity with the presence of God. It is where we become entwined with the record of His DNA. *"This mystery [of two becoming one] is great; but I am speaking with reference to [the relationship of] Christ and the church"* (Eph 5:32 AMP).

When we take communion, there are many depths and layers of the Kingdom realms connected to this process, with secrets to be uncovered that YHVH has for us as His sons *"God's glory is shown when He conceals things; a king's glory is shown in his ability to explore the facts of the matter"* (Proverbs 25:2 VOICE), and Jesus has for us as our Bridegroom, *"I am jealous over you with a jealousy that comes from God…I promised to give you to Christ, as your only husband. I want to give you as his pure bride"* (2 Corinthians 11:2 EXB).

I began to realize that I need to build a bridal chamber inside my heart. I was trying to deal with this from a spiritual perspective, whilst thinking about the natural perspective. To repeat, this is not sexual interaction with YHVH. The only human who was united with YHVH was Mary, but that was not sexual. The Bible says Holy Spirit overshadowed her (Luke 1:35). To overshadow means to brood, to cause vibration or frequency, to cause interruption in this world, to plant a record of a testimony inside her womb. Holy Spirit overshadowed Mary to wipe out every other overshadowing that had gone before Him. *"When people began being numerous on earth, and daughters had been born to them, the sons of God, looking at the women, saw how beautiful they were and married as many of them as they chose… The Nephilim were on earth in those days (and even afterwards) when the sons of*

God resorted to the women, and had children by them. These were the heroes of days gone by, men of renown" (Genesis 6: 1-2, 4 NJB). These were wrongful overshadowings. Where did they get that idea from? They got it from the garden.

Holy Spirit overshadowing is God's presence cleansing the generational seed line. It was about Holy Spirit and the glory of God overshadowing us. I began to do a study on overshadowing, the huppah, the cloud of the glory of God that came over Mount Zion when the children of Israel went up to the mountain and followed them in the wilderness, the fire, and the overshadowing of the presence of God over the peoples' lives.

"On the morning of the third day, there was thunder and lightning with a thick cloud on the mountain. There was a very loud blast from a trumpet ... all the people in the camp trembled. Then Moses led...the people out of the camp to meet God. ...Mount Sinai was covered with smoke, because the LORD came down on it in fire...and the whole mountain...trembled. ...Then Moses spoke...and...God answered him... Moses took the blood...and sprinkled... it on the people, saying, "This is the blood that begins...the...Covenant... which the Lord has made...with you.

...Moses...and seventy of the elders of Israel went up the mountain and saw the God of Israel. Under his feet was a surface...that looked as if it were paved with blue sapphire stones, and it was as clear as the sky [heavens]! These leaders...saw God. The glory of the Lord...came down [settled] on Mount Sinai, and the cloud covered it for six days. On the seventh day the LORD called to Moses from inside the cloud. To the Israelites...the glory of the Lord looked like a fire burning on top of the mountain. Then Moses went into the cloud..." (Exodus 19: 16-19, 24: 8-11, 16-18 EXB)

This cloud became a major focus for my life. I realized that YHVH wanted to bring me into the cloud of His presence, so that I could become one with Him and so that the cloud could brood over me (Genesis 1:2) and overshadow my life. I want the cloud of God's presence over my life, with the provision and protection He brings.

I do not want to hear people say, "Oh I got slimed today." We need to get into the bridal chamber. YHVH has given us ways of escape, but we do not understand these ways yet. The ways of YHVH are all about intimacy. Because we do not understand this particular way of God, we do not yet understand the provision that YHVH has given us in this way. The Lord in His Word says, *"Walk in my ways..."* (Zechariah 3:7 NKJV). To be in the cloud is a way of escape.

Out of my desire to engage the Kingdom and have the Father come and manifest Himself in me, I prepared a room that I felt would be welcoming to the cloud of the glory of God inside my heart. I used my imagination to build this room and the atmosphere in the room to be God-centred not self-focused.

In the mornings I would get up out of bed and begin to pray in the spirit and worship as I began to build this room and build a place of worship there as the Bible says, *"My house shall be called a house of prayer"* (Isaiah 56:7 NKJV). I wanted to build a house of prayer for the glory of God to manifest inside this place that I was building. This little canopy was where my God was going to come to meet with me. So I began to turn my desire to meet with Him. *"And the Spirit and the bride say, "Come!" (Revelation 22:17 NKJV).* I wanted to meet with the presence of the glory of God so that in that meeting place I could become one with His spirit, because I wanted Him to brood over me.

Mary said, *"Be it unto me according to your word"* (Luke 1:38 KJ2000). So I prayed, "Father, do unto me as you will." I did not know what He was going to do, because I did not have a grid for any of this. How many other people teach this?

I went through this process of praying, "Father, how does this all work? What does it mean to become one with your presence? How do I do this thing?" I drew on the record of becoming one in the cloud and on the dance floor. I have a record of being soaked in the glory, and of God's presence coming into my garden in the cool of the day inside my being, *"I have come into my garden, my sister, my [promised] bride"* (Song of Solomon 5:1 AMP). I have a record and I have already established a testimony, so that this is a meeting place where I am going to engage YHVH and YHVH is going to engage me.

I was there praying, "Father, I thank You that I can stand in this place and worship You and I make a conscious choice to say to You today, be it unto me as You will, Father. I totally and absolutely surrender to Your desire for my life." Then I heard the sound of a rushing wind come into my physical room. I started to freak out because I could feel this wind blowing around me. It seemed like it was in the room, but it actually was not, because my spirit man was in this other room, and what was manifesting in the Kingdom world was being revealed in the natural world.

I suddenly felt myself shift, and I was in the bridal chamber with the wind of God blowing all around me. I could feel the canopy of the mist. I felt this mist come around me and realized that the cloud of God had come into my room (1 Kings 8:11). I started to allow my desire to turn. I wanted to dissolve, I wanted to have the type of encounter I had when I was entwined with the DNA of God. I wanted to dissolve into the mist. I just wanted to become one with the atmosphere of the glory of God's presence that was inside the room.

As I gave myself to that desire, I did not dissolve into it. It began to dissolve into me and melt into my being. I felt it through the outside into the center of my spirit man. I felt the unity and again there was a "click" sound as everything came into alignment to the purpose of YHVH inside of me "...*And as the bridegroom rejoices over the bride, So shall your God rejoice over you*" (Isaiah 62:5 NKJV). I was there for probably three and a half or four hours just saying, "Wow...!" I was as drunk as a skunk. I came out of it and I was sitting on the edge of my bed saying, "Wow!" All I could say was, "Wow!" For about three hours. I was wide awake, but in a different world.

What I have found with YHVH is that once I have been somewhere with Him and know the way in, then I have to go and visit again. So I went through the process of going in repeatedly until the whole world of the Kingdom began to open up.

When I am one with the Father I am where the Father is. "*That they all may be one; just as You, Father, are in Me and I in You, that they also may be one in Us...*" (John 17:21 AMP).

If my Father is omnipresent, then I can be where my Father is. "*There is one God and Father of everything. ·He rules everything and is everywhere and is in everything [who is over all and through all and in all]*" (Ephesians 4:6 EXB).

If my Father is omnipotent and I am one with the Father, then I will be what my Father is. *"And [so that you will begin to know] what the immeasurable and unlimited and surpassing greatness of His [active, spiritual] power is in us who believe..."* (Ephesians 1:19 AMP).

If my Father is omniscient and I am one with the Father, then I will be what my Father is displaying. *"Call to Me and I will answer you, and tell you [and even show you] great and mighty things, [things which have been confined and hidden], which you do not know..."* (Jeremiah 33:3 AMP).

It all comes out of intimacy and out of the desire to build a realm of intimacy for the Father to engage us so we can engage the world and bring the Kingdom into this world to change it.

It comes out of the realm of intimacy and flows out of us like a river into the world, bringing divine order into everything that is around our lives. We want to be an extension of the Father's realm flowing through us to the world that is around us. The world wants to know about love. The Bible says, *"...everyone who loves is born of God and knows God. The one who does not love does not know God, for God is love"* (1 John 4:7-8 KJ2000). If YHVH is love then we need to learn how to love. We cannot love out of the stuff of physical life around us; we have to love out of that which YHVH made to flow from inside of us that becomes a river.

If we want to know about the life of a person we are talking with, then we can go and walk in the garden and go into the bridal chamber. Sitting in the bridal chamber and getting imbibed in the cloud of the mist of God, we can go and see what is in the life of a person, because whatever is in them is disposed and exposed to the presence of God.

Everything begins to open up in that place of intimacy. The whole Kingdom world begins to open up when we are in the presence of God, because we are seeing not from us into it but from Him into it, and so everything is made naked and plain to be seen. When we are engaged with the presence of God we have all the empowerment to deal with this, and we have all the glory of God to be revealed and to bring others into.

This was three years of my life. Do not expect to go into the bridal chamber and have this type of experience in one day and come out one day later with everything changed. The reality is that it takes work. Marriage is work; it takes work learning how to communicate. It takes work learning how to talk to one another about the difficult things, especially when the other one knows all the difficult things anyway, so how do we talk about the difficult things?

This is why the Bible says, *"let your requests be made known to God"* (Philippians 4:6 NKJV). But we do not make our needs known yet – we go in first and become one with Him, and in the expression of that oneness, then we say, "Father, this is my need." That is why the Bible says, *"come boldly to the throne of grace, that we may obtain mercy and find grace to help in time of need"* (Hebrews 4:16 NKJV). The need is always at the end. In the encounter, YHVH gives the provision for the sustenance of what is necessary to meet our needs. It is in the encounter, but we do not chase the encounter, we chase our Father, who releases us into encounter.

This is Kingdom work; this is good stuff and it really works. Everything that any one of us struggles with, we all struggle with. We all have the same DNA, the same fallen nature. But with it YHVH has made a way of escape. *"No temptation has overtaken you except such as is common to man; but God is faithful, who will not allow you to be tempted beyond what you are able, but with the temptation will also make the way of escape, that you may be able to bear it"* (1 Corinthians 10:13 NKJV). YHVH is giving us ways of escape, and this is one of my ways of escape, to go in and engage him in these areas of my life. When I am feeling alone, I go into my garden. When I am feeling desperate and in need of the touch of YHVH, I go into the Bridal Chamber. When I am feeling desperate and in need of changing, I go into the soaking room of preparation. I go into these places because I have gone in and out of them so many times that it is normal to be able to stand here and just step into the reality of that until it becomes a reality down here.

It should be normal for us to have access to our Father's Kingdom. This is just one little part of the provision that YHVH has given us, provision to meet our needs. It is all found in the realm of intimacy with His presence.

Activation

Father, I want to thank You that You have bought us as a bride.

You paid the price; You have supplied all that is needed out of Heaven and in Heaven, and in us, Father, to bring the fullness of Your Kingdom to bear on the earth.

Father, today we want to acknowledge that everything we do must stem out of a desire for intimacy with Your presence; not to chase experiences, but Father to chase You, the provider of the experiences.

Out of the platform of this relationship with You Father, show us Your Kingdom. It is Your pleasure Father, to show us Your kingdom. Father I ask that the atmosphere of the cloud of Your presence would rest over these men and women reading this book, that the shekinah glory of the omniscience of Your power would overshadow us in the night watch.

Father that You would change us, You would transform us, that in the night time we would engage Your presence and we would be found morning by morning Lord more in unity with Your presence.

Father, I thank You that You lead us and You guide us, and Father it is line upon line, precept upon precept, glory to glory, and that You are leading us into glory Father, to be revealed as sons on the earth in glory, in Heaven, fully manifesting the potential of what You have given to us here on the earth to live in.

Father, I thank You for grace. I thank You for great grace assigned to us, Lord, to engage the Kingdom world to see Your presence manifested and terraform the face of this universe, in Yeshua's mighty name. Amen.

CHAPTER 8

BUILDING A GARDEN IN YOUR HEART

In the previous chapter we looked at the four chambers of the heart, the bridal chamber, the soaking room, the dance floor and the garden in our heart. In this chapter I now want to teach more specifically about how to build the garden inside your heart.

God said, "Let the earth bring forth grass, the herb that yields seed, and the fruit tree that yields fruit...and it was so" (Genesis 1:11). YHVH said this before He created man in His image to work the ground (Genesis 1:26). The reality is that everything grew in Heaven first, and then came out of Heaven onto the earth as Adam and Eve brought it down. Of course everything was not in the state that it is in now. It was in an unfallen, totally harmonic, light, glorified, majestic state.

"And the LORD God planted a garden (oasis) in the east, in Eden (delight, land of happiness); and He put the man whom He had formed (created) there. And [in that garden] the LORD God caused to grow from the ground every tree that is desirable and pleasing to the sight and good (suitable, pleasant) for food ... Now a river flowed out of Eden to water the garden; and from there it divided and became four [branching] rivers ... the LORD God took the man [He had made] and settled him in the Garden of Eden to cultivate and keep it" (Genesis 2:8-10, 15 AMP).

The garden was man's entry into the earth to bring the glory of God, to subdue the earth and cultivate what was in Heaven on the earth. The glory of the Lord was the only thing on the face of the earth when YHVH made Adam. So Adam was not made out of dirt, he was made out of the glory dust of the presence of the glory of God. (Genesis 2:7)

It was a spiritual reality. Adam and Eve were all about the garden in Eden – that is why the garden was made, to put Adam and Eve there. Eden and the garden are not all one place because, *"...God planted a garden toward the east, in Eden..."* (Genesis 2:8 AMP). This is what the Bible says, but in Sunday school we are taught that it is the Garden of Eden – no, it is the garden *in* Eden. (You can read more about this in the chapter entitled 'Eden' in my first book, Realms of the Kingdom Volume 1.)

When Satan fell, the electrons on the outside of the nuclei of atoms began to form an elliptical pattern instead of a circular pattern. When something forms an elliptical pattern, the new vibration consistent with that form puts it out of harmony with its reality and the truth of the harmonious circular pattern of original creation. (By the way, Eve did not bite an apple, that is just a man-made idea, see Genesis 3:6.)

Then Adam and Eve sinned and came into collusion with what satan had done to make a seed line after their own kind, causing massive exchange so that the river from Eden (Genesis 2:10) was shut off. Today it is a spiritual river in a spiritual place connected into our spirit being. The river flowing through Eden still exists and I have seen and experienced it (see the chapter entitled 'The River' in Realms of the Kingdom Volume 1), but it connects into our spirit being. The only supply that would come to the earth would come through the belly of a person who stands in the realm of government, as the Word says, *"If anyone believes in me, rivers of living water will flow out from that person's heart (belly)..."* (John 7:38 EXB). Your spirit lives in the cavity in your brain and down your spinal column, in that little membrane that is held with cerebrospinal fluid and sits on the throne of your belly. Remember the law of first mention – the first mention of a river in the Bible is flowing from the seat of the government of our Father (Gen 2:10). For that river to come out of us we have got to be seated on the throne of government that YHVH has given us; and then out of our belly, from that place of government, will flow a river of living water. You and I are the ones that open up the realm of the capacity for the presence of God to water the earth, when we administrate the Kingdom.

What Father is looking for is the development of relational connection with Him deep in our inner being, so that we can come through that inner being to encounter and begin to walk with Him in the realm of the supernatural world.

But the problem is this: If the four heads of the river are not functioning within us, the water is not going to flow. So when we pray, "God, let the river flow out of our bellies!" YHVH replies, "I do not even know you – you want all the signs and wonders, but actually, I do not know you (Matthew 7:23). When was the last time you came visiting?" One time He asked me that question. He said, "Why do you love Me? *Why* do you actually love Me? What is your motive for loving Me? Is it to have spiritual experiences? Is it to get more from Me or to get brownie points? What is your motive?"

Every experience we have cannot just be about having an experience, it needs to be about engaging in intimacy with the God who brings us into those experiences – everything we do has to spring-board out of intimacy. We have too many people on the face of the earth today chasing spiritual experiences. Yes, spiritual experiences are wonderful things, but they should not be why we engage God.

It is about our role, function and responsibility to administrate what you and I engage with in the world of our Heavenly Father. It is about the processes you and I are engaged in and the realms that are associated with that responsibility there, manifesting down here. Out of our engagement and who we are in Him, the whole thing will begin to unlock for us so we can begin bringing what He needs to be mandated onto the face of the earth.

Visual Anchors for a Spiritual Reality

Part of my journey has been to try and build a place inside of me. Years ago I did not know that I had a garden in my heart. I just knew I had to find that place of fellowship with the presence of God inside of me where I could commune with Him, and try to spend time with Him deep inside of my being. YHVH stopped that access when Adam sinned, but in Christ YHVH gave us back that access and it can start as a garden in your life.

I am very visual and because there is a river I needed a visual anchor for a river. So I put myself into a number of different settings trying to get to grips with the understanding of what it would be like to have this river and to try and see it in the spirit realm.

In those days I used to see things in the spirit realm all the time but I did not have anchors for them, so I could never put things together in my understanding. One day I went to a beautiful place called Maraekakaho falls. It is a large waterfall with a very intense shaft of water that flows out of a crevice at the top and thunders down the side into a little 25 foot deep pool at the bottom. It is just the most remarkable place to be. I remember thinking, 'God this is beauty, the heavenly river must look like this'.

As I was sitting on the riverbank I remember thinking, 'Well Lord, I know I have got to have a river because wherever the river is there is life, and I need to come back into life.' So I knew that I had to find a river. So for about an hour I just watched the river and the leaves going past in the rushing stream.

I closed my eyes hearing the sounds of the water and meditated over what the heavenly river would be like. When I opened my eyes to look at the water, it was like something was changing, as degree upon degree upon degree of change began to take place and slowly it took shape into something totally different. At first I thought I was hallucinating, when I started transitioning into the reality of the supernatural world in and around the river that I desired; your heart's desire is powerful, as the Word says:

"...Delight yourself in ADONAI, and he will give you your heart's desire" (Psalm 37: 4 CJB).

The riverbank began to change and then the sound of the water began to sing to me, call me and desire for me to be in it and be one with it. It wanted to play with me and love on me. As I looked down I realized that the riverbank had begun to change as well. I was sitting on a rock and literally felt that the rock was trying to move around so it could embrace me. How do you explain that?

So I was busy looking at this river and thinking, 'Lord, which river is this? How do I fit this into my heart?'

The Lord said to me, "In every human heart there is a river, because out of your belly shall flow rivers of living water. In your life, in your garden, there is a river. This is what your river looks like". I began to see that on either side of the riverbank around me all the foliage had disappeared and it was just like desert sand. I started thinking, 'Lord I do not want desert sand. I wanted all the wonderful trees and all the things that were around here'.

The Lord said, "Yes that is fine, I want them too. The problem is you have not done anything about it."

I said, "Lord what do you mean, 'I have not done anything about it'?" I did not even know I had to do something.

He said, "Well, you have never asked". By then four hours had passed and I had to pull myself out of that realm and go home. So through the ensuing weeks I began a process every morning of going back to that same place in my mind, praying in tongues, engaging my spirit and drawing myself back into that place of engagement with the realm of the Kingdom of Heaven.

I would find that while in my room at home I would begin to step into that same place and I would see the same thing. Then I began to think, 'Well I have got to start growing things. But how do you grow things in the spirit?' I had no idea.

Growing your Garden

So the Lord said to me, "You have had many experiences that we need to celebrate together. These are the seeds that grow into trees". I started to take the seeds of some of the things that I had experienced with YHVH in my life. At times I have had victories over struggles where suddenly YHVH brought a change into my life. These were points of celebration for me. What better way to remember a celebration than to plant a seed that would grow into a tree. That tree would be the point of celebration. I am not worshiping the tree; I am just saying that the tree is the symbol of celebration of that life victory.

The Bible says, "...*What is the kingdom of God like? And to what shall I compare it? It is like a mustard seed, which a man took and planted in his own garden; and it grew and became a tree...*" (Luke 13:18-19 AMP). I said, "Lord I take this situation in my life as a seed, like a walnut seed, because the experience I had was very bitter and it was a very hard place I was in. But I know that a walnut tree is one of the most amazing trees to watch grow and the wood is just unbelievable.

So I took this walnut seed and said, "Lord by faith I stick this in the ground." I got some water and poured it over the seed, because you need to water the seed. Then again I took some more water and watered the seed. For days I seemed to be watering the seed. I said, "Lord how come it is not growing?"

He said, "Because you have not spoken to it yet".

Nobody tells you these things. So I took some water and I said to this experience, "Grow into a tree, grow!" YHVH wants to teach us how to create and you learn to create first deep inside your own being. So I spoke to this nut. "Grow, grow; in the name of Jesus grow." I turned around to get more water, and suddenly there was the tree. It was the most remarkable tree that I had ever seen in my life. The leaves were singing the victory that I had planted the tree to celebrate, whispering with the wind of YHVH blowing in them. It was whispering victory and singing to me: "How amazing it is to stand with you in this place of victory!"

I thought that was so amazing that I decided to go and plant another one and another and another. I was so focused on doing it that I built a forest around one side of this bank. The Lord said to me, "You have been working around here so well, but what about the rest of it"?

I said, "How much more is there?" He replied, "Well you have not looked yet". In the spirit realm you only notice logical things. There was a rise on the edge of the riverbank and I had never gone beyond what I was doing there. I would go there and I would begin to stand and worship in the Spirit in the middle of this garden that I had planted, feeling the presence of YHVH. I did not want to be anywhere else but where the presence of YHVH was. I would feel His presence come into that place and I would begin to worship Him, and we would talk about a lot of things in my own life.

So I turned around and thought, 'Well I need to go and take a look at what is over the bank'. It is amazing how curious we humans are. We always need to see the other mountain, that mountain over there. So I climbed the bank and there was an amazing bowl shaped valley of about eight or nine acres. I said, "Lord this is too big for me to fill with plants".

He said, "I am not asking you to plant it. I am asking you to speak it into being".

Speaking Life into Being

We are called to speak and to learn how to create with our words. As the Bible shows us, *"And God said, "Let there be..."* (Genesis 1:3 AMP), *"Death and life are in the power of the tongue, and those who love it will eat its fruit"* (Proverbs 18:21), *"...God who gives life to the dead and calls into being that which does not exist"* (Romans 4:17 AMP).

I love daffodils; they are amazing flowers to me. When they come up in my garden in the spirit realm they have wonderful green stems; then a green thing makes a whooshing sound out of the middle and has a nice little yellow flower on it that follows the sun. In my nation (New Zealand) we have fields of daffodils. When I was a kid I used to love running through the daffodils, because you would get them caught between your toes. And if you fell over you could roll on the leaves and you would not get hurt because there were so many of them. You could also lie down in the daffodils and no one could see you. I used to bring my line of sight so that I could just see over the top of the daffodils to this layer of absolute bright yellow across the field. To me as a kid that was amazing.

In my mind I was thinking, 'Lord I would like a field of daffodils, just like we have at home'.

He said, "Well just speak it out". So I said, "Father in the name of Jesus I speak to this ground, *'Grow'* daffodils." Then I heard a whirlwind sound. It was the wind of YHVH that came out of my mouth. If we are God-like beings then we carry the breath of life to create. As we read, Jesus *"...breathed on them, and said to them, "Receive the Holy Spirit"* (John 20:22). He did more than just give them the Holy Spirit. So as the breath came out of me, it became the breath of God, not that I am God but that is the way God works. If you do your part, then He will do His part.

Then suddenly the field grew all these daffodils and the sound they made was the sound of singing. They were worshipping the presence of YHVH. To me there is no better place than to sit in the middle of a field with flowers worshipping YHVH.

I did not want to break any of them. In the natural world as you walk along and brush against a stem the flower falls over and is broken. That is why I used to love running because you would break them between your toes and you would come out with toes full of daffodils. So I was really carefully stepping around these. I remember bumping into one of the flowers and thinking, 'Oh no, it is going to break and die'. But of course in the realm of the Kingdom there is no death. So when I brushed past this daffodil, bending the stem, all it did was spring back up again. Then I started to wonder if these daffodils could break and as I tried, the whole plant went "boing" and came back up again. I said, "Hallelujah! I can run through this". Then I ran through them and actually tripped and rolled through the daffodil paddock with the daffodils pushing me around as if I was crowd surfing, while the daffodils were singing and glorifying YHVH.

It took me a number of years to grow different places in my garden that would be places of celebration for the experiences of my life. Some of the places I have built are very quiet places. Some of them are very loud 'in your face' places. Some of them are sanctuaries that I have built because of the sanctuary that YHVH has become to me in my life. Every time I go into the realm of the spirit and something happens there I go and plant a seed. I have forests that I have planted and I can go there in a fraction of time to draw back to that place inside my heart to experience the presence of YHVH in any one of those places because I have chosen to build a garden of intimacy with Him there.

"The LORD God... put the man [or Adam;] in the garden of Eden to care for [or till] it..." (Genesis 2:15 EXB). So I have tilled the ground of my heart so that the rain, the presence and the voice of YHVH could come into the ground of my heart.

I did not realize that this garden was in the midst of Eden. The same way as YHVH put a garden in Eden, this garden that I had grown was in Eden, which gave me direct access to the person of YHVH when He is off the throne (see the chapter entitled "Eden" in Realms of the Kingdom Volume 1). I realized that I now have a garden in the midst of Eden. Not only that but I have a river that flows into the river of God; and the river of God grows bigger as my river adds into the tributaries of the rivers from other gardens that all flow into the river of YHVH that comes from the throne. Your river adds to God's river and part of you is going to flow through it into the earth, producing life wherever it goes. It is all about us – YHVH, you and me all doing something together because we are enabled to. That is what Adam and Eve were made for – to go and multiply, reproduce, subdue and take care of this creation.

In Eden

One of the things I learnt to do was to walk in my garden and realize that I could go from my garden, step into God's garden and start to tend to some of His garden. God's garden, Eden, is amazing. Heaven is just an unbelievable place (I go into more detail on this in my audio teaching "Walking in Eden" available from my website: www.sonofthunder.org

There are some things in Eden that I think would be really good for me to teach you about. As you go along one of the pathways into Eden there is an orange blossom tree that has blossom and oranges on it. You are a spirit being in this realm, so gravity is not an issue. You can walk in and amongst the blossom and fruit in the trees. The blossoms sing and all they do is look for the person of YHVH to come past. They wait for Him the same way as we wait upon the Lord. That is all they do. You can eat them as well, because you are a spirit being and they are spiritual entities. There is life in anything you take and eat. You can eat of the trees that are in Eden and the most amazing thing is you can pick an orange and take a bite out of it. Then if you leave it there it does not fall to the ground, it will stay there and wait for you to come back and finish it.

In the garden there are white fruit trees that have silver woven into them. But we can go and feed them with the river that is in you. It is like laying hands on people; you can lay hands on the roots of the trees and release the anointing to grow the fruit of your life in Eden. Then what is in your life passes into the tree and that is the fruit that grows. You can then go and eat the fruit of your life. There are others that have gone in there before us and we can eat some of the fruit of their lives as well. You can taste and see the God that is in them. Not only can you taste and see it but also you can begin to experience some of what they had in YHVH. How do you come into the realms that another has walked in? You go and eat some of the fruit.

In my day job I used to spend much of my time doing mundane things like mowing the lawn. I used to love mowing the lawns because I could get myself locked into the realm of the spirit walking around with a really small lawn mower, so it would take me hours to mow an acre of ground. I am the boss of a complex of swimming baths in New Zealand but I would walk around mowing the lawn to use a mundane thing to cause my spirit man to encapsulate what YHVH had been doing and then lock myself into it. So for an hour while I was mowing the lawns I would be walking in the spirit as well doing things in the presence of YHVH.

These things became very important to me. I would spend my days doing that, until it flowed into the night watch (see chapter 1) because I had chosen to do something about what YHVH had spoken to me to do.

Healing in the Spirit Realms

I shared this with a youth group around twenty years ago, and one of these girls whose hands were riddled with arthritis said to me, "Ian I want to till the ground but I cannot move my hands". I said to her, "You do not need your hands when you are there; you are a spirit being so you are able to do it." She came back the next morning and showed me that her hands had been completely healed, because she had chosen to go and touch the water. In transferring the water YHVH had healed her hands. Nobody had to go and lay hands on her. YHVH had done it because she had chosen to go and do something about what YHVH had shown her. To me this is miracle stuff. It is not about someone else praying for us; this is about the places of intimacy that we are invited to develop.

We all need to develop the lion and the lamb within us. Too

many people have the lamb and not enough lion. Others have too much lion and not enough lamb inside of them. What YHVH is looking for is the nature of the Lamb of God, who is Jesus, inside of us, together with the Lion of Judah empowering your soul, and for both of them to lie down together in absolute unity and adoration of the One who made you. When you die your spirit returns to YHVH. It is your spirit that keeps you alive on Earth. How much influence your spirit has had on your soul is going to dictate the measure of the glory that is going to manifest in your soul when you die.

When our spirit man is becoming active it is transforming our soul into its image, and the image of my spirit is the image of Jesus, the Son of God. The more my spirit encounters the presence of YHVH, the greater the image my soul is going to take on that image. To the point where I do not have to die because my body is taking on the image of my soul, my soul is taking on the image of my spirit and my spirit has the image of the Son in it already.

I would do this in secret because whatever you do in secret YHVH will show openly for others to see. People would ask me what was going on with me because they could see something changing in my life. I had gone through inner healing and deliverance, but I needed to grow something back in that place. The garden inside your heart is a fantastic place to start growing a relationship with the presence of YHVH in your inner being. If you want to become a God-like being you need to begin to grow a relationship with YHVH inside of you, so that you take on the image of the one you are fellowshipping with, on the inside.

The garden became a very important place for me to walk in and go into. I still go back there and do things, like plant a tree of remembrance, so every time I go there I see that this is what I did that day. I do this in the night watch. That is why the night watch is so important, because I can spend eight hours there with YHVH.

Intimacy with the Lord

It is important for us to realize that there is more to being a believer than just doing the religious stuff we have always been taught. There is a whole realm of intimacy in a personal deep relational way that YHVH wants to bring to the church. It is all about you desiring Him and building a desire for Him, to want to know Him, understand Him and share His life with Him. It is only as you desire these things that you will get known as a friend of YHVH. It was important for me to hear YHVH say, "Ian you are my friend".

It is your choice; YHVH will not over ride your will. He knows where you choose to spend your life, just like I know most of the things that my children are doing and where they are at, because I can see them and I do all these things around them. But I love it when they come in and tell me, and I say, "That's wonderful, that's great." It builds interactive intimacy and relational communion, one with another. That is what YHVH wants with us, He wants that intimacy and relational connection of being one with you.

The greatest part about all of this is that when you build relationship with Him here inside your heart, you then have a right to go into His presence there in His kingdom and He will welcome you in the courtrooms; He will welcome you in and around the throne. You build the intimacy here inside of you, which gives you the right to go there. If you have not built the intimacy here, you will find the throne a terrifying place, because He is different when He is on the Throne from when He is in other places.

The Bible says Adam and Eve "*...heard the sound of the LORD God walking in the garden...*" (Genesis 3:8). A voice does not have footsteps. It was a conscious awareness of the arrival of a measure of anointing or the arrival of a person. I can be praying at home and be aware of the arrival of someone with a measure of anointing as I hear a knock on my door. I will be aware before they even get there, because you become aware of the atmosphere. Whatever a person carries goes into the atmosphere. It is that atmosphere you carry that enables others to be aware of who you are. So what Adam felt was the atmosphere that YHVH carried, as he became aware that He had walked into the garden.

The voice was saying, "Adam where are you? I love you. I have spent this time talking with you, son, I love you, where are you?" There are times when I would try and hide from YHVH, playing hide and seek, standing beside some trees to watch Him, because I love watching the way YHVH moves. I love the way He walks and the majesty, the stature, the assurance, and the complete absolute self-confidence of His being. He is *"I Am who I Am"* (Exodus 3:14).

I love watching Him when He goes past because He is totally aware of me, I am totally aware of Him and it is fun. What YHVH is looking for is relationship. With everything you do He is looking for relationship. It means more to Him than giving you all the power of the Kingdom. He wants intimacy, to know you and be known by you. It only comes out of doing some of these things and spending the time with Him. I would really encourage you to find the place inside of your being where the presence of God is, and to begin to commune with it.

He will talk with you and enable you to come and do some of these things. It took me about three years to learn the process of doing this. I have dug channels leading from the river in my garden. I love ponds and small lakes. I love sitting on the edge of a lake and watching the water. Often the Spirit of God will move, and sometimes when I am sitting next to the water I will see the water begin to move and I will know that Holy Spirit has turned up to come and speak with me. I have got this little eddy that runs away from the stream and I built a little lake, and that is where I go and commune with Holy Spirit by that lake. I wait for Him to move the face of the water. Then I know He is coming, so I will close my eyes and I will become enveloped in His presence. These little things have built in me an assurance and an awareness that YHVH loves me and I just do not care what the church has to say. I just do not care. They can call me a spirit freak, but I do not care. I know I have a relationship with the person of YHVH. That to me is sweeter than anything. I have had the Lord speak to me in the throne room around other people saying, "Son come here." To be called a son by YHVH in the throne room is totally affirming.

I would encourage you when you go to bed to begin to lock into the presence of God. Meditate and think on the things that have touched or inspired you in this chapter. *"Finally, believers, whatever is true, whatever is honorable and worthy of respect, whatever is right and confirmed by God's word, whatever is pure and wholesome, whatever is lovely and brings peace, whatever is admirable and of good repute; if there is any excellence, if there is anything worthy of praise, think continually on these things [center your mind on them, and implant them in your heart]* (Philippians 4:3 AMP). Allow your mind and your heart to be captivated with this potential. YHVH will share His kingdom with you but He wants to share His life with you first. When you can get His life then you will get the Kingdom.

Activation

One of the key things that empowers me to go into the realm of the presence of God is the blood of Christ and knowing that the blood has empowered me to bring me to the point of righteousness and holiness. This gives me access into the realm of the presence of God, and it is through that blood that I come. It is not through my own efforts, it is through the blood of Christ. It is the blood that cleanses me, it is the blood that makes me whole, it is the blood that makes me righteous.

"Father, I want to thank You that you have made a way into the realm of your Kingdom. Father, thank You that there is a way for us to walk in Your presence and according to Your Word, Father, it says there that you caused a garden to grow. You grew all the herbs of the fields and You made a place Lord, where You would begin to fellowship with Adam.

Father, tonight I want to thank You that what was in Adam, in that day, has been given back to us in Christ. Father, in the cool of the day, which is the beginning of the new day, which is evening, which is where we are now, it says that You came walking in the garden in the cool of the day, calling out Adam's name.

Father, I want to thank You that You are calling my name, You are calling me into relationship with Your presence. Father, I thank You that there is a river that flows from Your throne. According to Your Word, Father, that river flows through Eden, waters the garden which is my heart, and from there it waters the face of the earth. Father, I thank You for the river of Your presence. Thank You Lord that the river is a cry and a desperation inside Your heart for friendship, for relationship and for intimacy with us as Your children.

Father, today I make a choice to enter the realm of Your presence by the blood of Jesus Christ. Father, I engage the realm of Your presence today, and Lord, I make a choice to stand beside the river of life that flows within me as a great gushing river. Father, I hear the cry of Your call for intimacy, relationship and friendship and I turn my ear and I turn my heart towards that desire for You and with You today. It is coming out of Your heart. It is coming out of Your place in the realm of the throne.

Father, I turn to the river You have given me, Father, with the grass, with the sand that moves and is alive, with all the stones and the gems that move in the sand and the grass that looks and smells and moves with the wind, and the voice of Your presence. Father, I see the river that is amazing in its clarity, full of gold, full of diamonds, full of stones, full of absolute beauty.

Father, from the past, when I have stood in that river it has been amazing to feel it flow through me, and today I just walk by faith into that river. I walk into the place where Your voice and the river of Your glory flows through my body, through my soul, through my spirit, washing me, cleansing me, speaking to my DNA, calling me into relationship and intimacy with Your presence. Lord I know that You are standing on the bridge, way down there, but Father it is fascinating to watch the river move with the Your voice, and the scrolls of the fish that move inside the testimony of the water.

Father, the trees that cast forth their leaves are for the healing of the nations (Revelation 22:2). Father, thank you that these leaves are living things that move in the water like schools of fish. Father, today I choose to walk up the river, to bury my head into it just like Ezekiel did (Ezekiel 47). Lord, I desire to have it over the top of my head, to be able to be buried into the voice of YHVH. Lord I lean into the voice of Your presence, I lean into the realm of Your presence. Lord, I allow my desire to begin to turn towards Your glory and towards Your presence. Father, today I just walk up off the edge of the bank, and I walk down beside the pathway, heading towards the bridge where I know You are standing.

Jesus I thank You that You are my Lord, I thank You that You died for me, You made a way for me to come to get to know the Father. You made a way to bring me back to this place of encounter with Your Father. Jesus thank You that You are the Son of God.

Thank You that You died, to totally and absolutely redeem me from every mark, every record, every iniquity, every transgression and every sin.

Lord, today I open up my heart and ask You to reach into my heart and remove the record of that enmity that has fought against You and fought against the Father's desire for my life. Jesus I know that no sin, no record of sin can enter the realm of the Father, and willingly I yield to Your administration and Your hand to reach into me, to take out of me the record of the stain of my sin. Jesus thank You that You are my burden bearer. Thank You Lord that You work with me and You walk with me, You talk with me, and You work in me to deal with this stuff.

Thank You Lord that today I can stand totally and absolutely free because You paid the price to reach into me. Jesus, thank You that You have given me a new heart. Thank You Jesus that You have given me a new record in my body; a new testimony of Your presence. Jesus I know that You are my brother, but I can hear the voice of the Father calling. I can hear Him calling, and Lord I allow my heart to respond to Your word and to Your presence, and I turn into the light of Your glory. The countenance of Your presence that shines over the places in Eden. I turn into that realm of the glory of God today. I give myself to the Father, I give my desires, and I give all my longings over to the Father.

Lord, I just want to be with You today. I just want to hang and be around You and watch what You do. Lord I know that I have met You by the rose garden, and today I just choose to walk along the path that leads down into that little valley by the rose garden, and I know You are there because I can hear You snipping the roses again. Father, to see You, to know that You are here, and to know that I am standing with You, is an amazing thing.

Father, thank You that You love me. Thank You Lord that You never gave up on me. Thank You, Father, that even when I was yet in sin, You held on believing that this day would come when I can stand here with You, walking with You and talking with You, Father.

Lord I thank You for the flowers that You have made. These most amazing things that appear out of nowhere, that out of the realm of who You are as a Father, You knit together Your purpose, You knit together Your desires, You knit them together, completely and wonderfully made.

Father, thank You for Your call on my life. Thank You Lord for who You have called me to be as a son. Thank You Lord that Your one desire is for me to be with You in Your garden, to spend time here engaging Your presence and being with You. Father, today I turn to the realms that You have opened up here Lord down by the mountain of gold, by the mountain of Your glory where the eagles cry, where they welcome Your presence into this place; Father to the sand and the ground that is around us, to the grass and the birds, to the sounds of the wind of YHVH that is moving in the trees as the angels watch.

Father, thank You that it is a privilege to be able to stand here with You today. Lord, today I receive, I thank You that You are my friend, I do not know how to build relationship with You in this intimate way Father, but I set my heart to want to become Your friend. I want to know You, Father, I want to know who You are, I want to know what You do, I want to know why You do it and how You do it. Lord, I want to watch You do it, and Lord what I see You do I would choose to do also.

Father, I thank You that in this place there are many Lord that have walked in the realm of your presence, and I know that You are calling to each one of them Father.

I ask Lord that You would become their shepherd, that You would watch over them Father as a shepherd watches over the sheep. For each one, Father, I ask that You would engage them and encounter them, that Your love and that Your glory Father, flow over them. Lord, that they would be changed. Lord and that they would experience and understand the height and depth and breadth of their calling (Ephesians 3:18).

Father, I thank You for the new things that You have made here in this garden. Lord, the new trees that You have planted for me, because of the things that I have walked and the victories that we have walked together, the trees that have grown and recorded the testimony of the things that we have done. Father, thank You for those records, I see them in Your garden, that they hold true to who You are, that You are a God that remembers the good things. The God that remembers the victories, and I choose that today Father. I choose to see those things that You remember.

Lord, I thank You that I can love You in this place and appreciate and honour the relationship with You here, outside of Your throne. Father, thank You; Father thank You.

Thank You for the new things, Father. Thank You for the precious fragrances that You have generated and made, here in the garden. Father, thank You for the fragrances that speak of Your love for me. Thank You for the fragrances, Lord, that speak of the purifying and the cleansing of Your beauty, Your presence within and around my life. Thank You, Lord, that everything speaks of Your wonder, everything speaks of Your glory.

Father, I appreciate and honour You today. I honour You Lord and I bow down and worship You today, as my Father. The seed that I carry is of You today. I ask You to reach into me Father and change the record of the seed. You change the record of my heart, You change my inner man, Father, You can change me, You translate me, and Father You transform me, to be able to carry a different record from the realm of Your presence.

Father, I thank You that this is a place I can come to again and again, and You never, ever get bored with me. Thank You Lord that I can find friendship here. Thank You, Lord, that I can sit on the mountains and look over the beauty of Your creation and the secret things that You have made.

Father, I thank You for the realm that operates out of this atmosphere of Your presence, where we can create if we watch and see. Father, thank You that You are a God of creation, a God that just loves to make things. I thank You for the new things You have made, in this atmosphere of the place of Your glory, in Eden, Father.

Lord, today I need to go, Lord, I just want to thank You that I have been able to spend some time Lord, just to spend some time with You, in Your presence again. Lord, to be able to walk with You, to be able to be next to You Father. Lord, I want to thank You for that. Lord, as I back away I allow my heart to yearn towards You, I allow my heart to turn towards You. Father, I love

You. Father I so value, I so appreciate You, I so value who You are and what You have become. Father, as I turn and as I back away from Your presence Lord, I will be back, I will come back and fellowship and speak with You tonight Father.

Lord, I want to thank You that You will wait, and You will wait for me, forever waiting as a father yearning after his sons, forever waiting for me to respond and come into the realm of Your presence. Father, thank You that You have brought me here today. Lord, as I back away I say "Lord I will be back tonight, I will see You later on tonight Father." Lord, as I back away from You today, Lord I turn as I get around the corner, I turn and Jesus I see You looking at me again with that knowing smile.

Jesus, thank You, thank You for what You have done for me to bring me back into relationship with the Father. Thank You that You have brought me back to this place.

Thank You Jesus that You have made it open for me to come back and fellowship with my Father here. Jesus, thank You, I so value and so appreciate what You have given to me. You have given me a gift of life, and I thank You that you are restoring me back into relationship with the Father.

Lord, I thank You for what You have given me, for what You have taken from me, for what You have yielded out of my life as fruit.

Lord, today I bow down and I worship You Jesus. I ask You to put Your hand on my head and bless me as a son. Jesus, I thank You that You are my friend. I have longed after You, I have sought after You and I have come to know You as a friend, I have come to know You as my Lord, I have come to truly know You as my saviour Jesus, thank You.

Lord, as I back away today Lord, I turn into the river that carries the voice of the Father. I go into the river Father and I choose to lie in the river, to move down, enveloped in the love of the Father. The tears are the expression of the joy of my God and my King woven into the river of glory. Father, as I float down the river, Father, I can hear Your voice calling, I hear You wooing Father with the promise to me to be back, to move my way down the river, to engage this realm of this atmosphere of the earth again.

Father, I come down the waterfall of Your presence, to move out of the atmosphere of Your glory, in the realm of eternity, and to fall down back onto the face of the earth into this realm, into this atmosphere.

Father, I thank You that I have been able to walk with You today. Thank You, Lord, that I have been able to see You and engage You. Lord, my desire is to become a friend of YHVH. Lord, I ask that You would plant a tree in memory of what I have done here today. Lord, every time I come calling You have planted a forest and record of the memory of what we have done here. Father, I ask You to plant a new tree, that when I come tonight, that I would see it as a memorial of my time with You here today.

Father, thank You that You love me, I so value You, Jesus I value You, Holy Spirit I really appreciate what You have done, in opening my heart, my eyes and my spirit man to engage the Father. Holy Spirit, thank You, thank You that You came willingly, when the Son ascended into the realm of the Father, You came willingly to engage me down here, to bring me into relationship with the Son and with the Father. Thank You Holy Spirit; thank You Lord.

Father, I ask that Your grace would come over us here today as a group of people. Father, wherever these people are Lord, I ask that Your Kingdom and the realm of Your presence would begin to draw them back to this place. Father, it has been awesome to meet with You, it has been awesome to be in the atmosphere of Your presence, awesome just to be around You and hang with other people Father, of Your Kingdom.

Hallelujah Jesus.

(Wherever you are I just want you to begin to make choices, to begin to withdraw quietly from where you are and whatever you are doing. One thing I have learnt to do is never to hurry when backing out of the presence of YHVH, but just to enjoy the kind of final touches, the final fragrances of just knowing and of being with the Father. I always just take my time backing out of His presence.)

Lord I want to thank You for Your grace, I want to thank You for Your love for me as a son. You did all this for me, I so appreciate that today, I so value it, Father, in the name of Jesus.

CHAPTER 9

HEAVENLY TRADING

In this chapter I want to teach about trading in the heavens and things that we can trade with because who you are in the heavens is who you are on the earth.

Jesus Tore the Veil

In front of me and around me is a veil that separates me from the realm of the Kingdom of Heaven. The Bible says that Jesus tore the veil (Matthew 27:51). This side of the veil is all that is in darkness and chaos. Through the veil is glory, light and absolute divine order, which is in His presence. *"Therefore, brothers and sisters, we have boldness to enter into the Holies by the blood of Yeshua. He inaugurated a new and living way for us through the curtain – that is, His flesh"* (Hebrews 10:19-20 TLV). It is not the place or the Person, but it is in His presence. The presence of God is not the Person of God. It is like taking a sniff and saying, "I can smell smoke." You know there is a fire because you can smell smoke. The presence of God is like the smoke from the fire of God. We can step through the veil into the presence of God because Jesus has torn that veil open for us. It just requires faith.

Practise

I practised this for twenty-one days, praying, "Father, by faith, I step into Your presence, into the realm of the Kingdom and I stand in Your presence. I come through that veil and stand in it. And then Father, I ascend up and down". He who walks up and down is wise. *"So I will strengthen them in the LORD, And they shall walk up and down in His name," Says the LORD"* (ZECHARIAH 10:12), *"You are the anointed cherub that covers; and I have set you so: you were upon the holy mountain of God; you have walked up and down in the midst of the stones of fire"* (Ezekiel 28:14 KJ2000).

If you walk up and down then you can teach others, which is what you are supposed to do. Stepping in, "Father now I ascend by faith into the place of Your presence. Now Lord, I move into the place of the government of Your presence. I engage that and I descend out of the place of Your presence. I descend from Your presence and I step with that onto the face of the earth. As a son I deliver that presence of Heaven onto the face of the earth, and I administrate onto the earth what I have engaged and brought out of Heaven". You do not draw it down. You go in and you bring it down. That is heavenly trading.

How to Trade

Trading in the heavens is about you going into His presence, engaging all the provision that He has, bringing it down here, and releasing it in its fullness around your life. So if you want to change an atmosphere you can feel in the spirit, you get a hundred people going in, engaging and going up into the place of His government, engaging the governmental realm of Heaven, engaging what is operating inside there, and then coming down. Each one brings that here onto the face of the earth, standing and beginning to release that into the atmosphere of the earth. That is how you do warfare. You do not need to go at every demon. But that is mainly what the church has been taught, because few people have taught us how to administrate Heaven on the earth. We are administrators of Heaven – trading into the realms of Heaven to engage what has already been rightfully given to us in Christ, to be able to administrate it down here on the face of the earth, *"Also, he has put all things under his feet and made him head over everything for the Messianic Community, which is his body, the full expression of him who fills all creation"* (Ephesians 1:22-23 CJB).

When you go in, you trade. The moment you go in, court protocol as we see in Zechariah 3 takes place (see The Courtroom of God chapter in Realms of the Kingdom Volume 1). You step into the presence of God and through Christ become righteous. That alone will change your life if you did that every day. "I come into Your presence and I stand fully righteous, fully holy, fully sanctified, fully made whole by being in Your presence. Lord, I lay hold of that fullness, step into this earth with that fullness, and I administrate it around my life into the atmosphere, every circumstance, every crevice and cavity and every hidden place of my life. I administrate what I have engaged in the presence of God in full righteousness here on the face of the earth." That is going to be better than "Father, I bind this thing and that thing operating in my life." That is good when you are a baby Christian and you need to do that. But YHVH wants us to become sons who administrate Kingdom victory, not sons who go around *just battling the demonic*. God does not want that. He wants us to mature and put away childish things (1 Corinthians 13:11). The problem is that most of the church has not matured yet. And the reason is because very few people have told us that only battling the demonic is wrong.

YHVH wants to manifest Himself on the earth and you are His gate to reveal Himself through. That is trading, as we simply pray, "Lord, I am a broken vessel in my flesh. Your Word says I am a gate so I can come into Your presence, and as I come into Your presence You can manifest Yourself through me because I am a gate to Your presence" (Psalm 24:7-9). Effective warfare is not focusing on demons but walking with YHVH, worshiping in tongues, bringing the Kingdom as it is in Heaven onto the earth.

Protocol of Transitional Relationship with YHVH

Holy Spirit is a friend and we need to learn how to develop a relationship with Him to then understand about developing relationship with Jesus, and then develop a relationship with the Father – because each one leads to the other. But before we can develop a relationship with Holy Spirit, Jesus has got to become Lord of our lives, not just Saviour. I had two different experiences with the Holy Spirit and the presence of Jesus. One was when I got my fire insurance and said, "Jesus, forgive me. I am a sinner." The other was, "Now Jesus has become Lord of my life" – two totally different experiences. Once He becomes Lord of your life, you can then learn out of His Lordship how to develop relationship, otherwise you are still doing your own thing which is like spiritual 'thumb sucking'.

The relational protocol of transition is trading – you develop relationship with Holy Spirit. Holy Spirit then wants you to develop relationship with Jesus. Holy Spirit backs off so you can trade His relationship into Jesus. Then you develop brotherhood relationship with Jesus and He becomes your brother as well as your Lord, your King, and your Saviour. Then He trades all that in so you can develop relationship with the Father. The Father teaches, trains and matures you. Then He trades His position and presents you to the world saying, "There is My son; when he is talking, I am talking; when he is moving, I am moving. He is My mouthpiece, listen to him." The Father trades His position. He never loses it, He trades it, because He wants you to become His fully fledged son so you carry His true reflection as it is in Heaven and has been in the Father's plan right from the Garden (Genesis 1:26-27).

Names of God are our Provision
YHVH is our provision. Every time we struggle with an area of provision or finances we need to engage YHVH for His provision for our life and look to Him regardless of how it comes. Your spirit man must be engaged with the names of God including Jehovah Jireh, Jehovah Nissi, and Elohim. I am the Lord your God, your Provider. You must engage His Names, and the Names are only found in the spirit realm in His Kingdom. When you turn into it, the supply of all His names is there for you. But you must engage them to set up a tone and a vibration in your being so your spirit, soul, and body come into the right tone of the supply of that Name. That is why speaking Hebrew is powerful. The Hebrew language matches our DNA vibration. Each strand of human DNA matches one single sound of the Hebrew language. When they play the tone to the DNA it straightens out and becomes what it should have been. That is what monatomic element does. It gets on either side of the DNA and produces a current through the DNA, which brings it back to its former memory.

Trading Floors

YHVH wants us to engage this issue of trading. When I went to Africa the Lord laid on my heart the full revelation of a whole lot of bad things I had traded. I love going to Africa. It is where I was born. I went to Namibia and I sat in the desert in Namibia for a day in the dirt, feeling the vibration, and the frequency of the first creation to understand the desire of YHVH to restore everything.

The Lord began to speak to me. First of all He began to convict me, because without repentance you have got nothing to turn from and you do not understand how much you have sinned and hurt the heart of YHVH. That is why the cross is so important. The blood and the cross of Christ have got to be central to our whole life and walk with YHVH. We need them; they are our two primary trading floors.

I began to realise that the enemy had copied a whole load of things. As it is in Heaven he has copied it so that he can present his own realm to people, who then buy into it unknowingly, because he always does this in darkness.

I started to pray, "Father try me and see and behold in me if there be any wicked thing in me, that You would empower me to become a son because I want Your glory to reside in me. I want to take on the new body You have promised me. I want it so that my DNA can begin to reflect Your glory. I take the DNA of the Son of God in the body and blood of Jesus, as Your Word says, *"Whoever has been born of God does not sin, for His seed remains in him; and he cannot sin, because he has been born of God"* (1 John 3:9). So I want that Scripture manifested in my life, and I want all this junk that is in my DNA out".

And the Lord said to me, "If you have done it one percent, you have done it Ian."

"Well, yes, I know that, Lord."

He said, "No, no, you are not hearing what I am saying. All the times that you have served in the church with the possibility that you may be made full-time ministry staff because you serve the church, the carrot was hung in front of your face and you gave your life, sowing into that manipulation. You were subject to a different trading floor".

When the Lord presented this to me, I thought, 'Oh, dunghill! I have got so much hanging over my life now I have got to repent'. When I shared it with the group that I mentor I was still in the middle of it and I said to them, "Listen, this is what YHVH is doing with me and He is going to do with you what He has done with me, because as the head is, so shall the body be.

I started the process, and then the Lord said, "Oh, good. Let's deal with a few more, shall we?" And so He started to speak to me about other trading floors in the demonic world: Tyre, Athaliah, Jezebel, Cain, Delilah, Leviathan and Apollyon. When I uncovered all this I spent six weeks repenting as the Lord began to speak to me about the garbage that was in my life. I thought I was clean; I did not realize just how much garbage I had stored inside my soul.

To understand 'trading floor' we need to understand what happened in the natural world to give us a blueprint of what occurs in the spirit world. *"Then Jesus went into the temple of God and drove out all those who bought and sold in the temple, and overturned the tables of the money changers and the seats of those who sold doves"* (Matthew 21:12). That was the first time since the fall of Adam that the spirit of mammon had been challenged on its trading floor.

YHVH began to speak to me about these seven trading floors, and I want look at them, starting with the unholy tri-unity that developed in Israel with Ethbaal, whose daughter was Jezebel, who married the King of Israel. *"Now Ahab... evil in the sight of the LORD ...he took as wife Jezebel the daughter of Ethbaal, king of the Sidonians; and he went and served Baal and worshiped him"* (1 Kings 16:30-31).

Ethbaal's granddaughter was Athaliah who married the King of Judah. These unholy alliances brought the issue of control over worship, limited financial freedom and controlled the army. So let us just talk about these three first of all because they are an unholy tri-unity that works together.

I spent weeks starting to go through the influence of the King of Tyre in my life. The King of Tyre is a demon spirit, symbolised in a man, who takes finances away from the church. Whenever you sow finances into a trading floor that is not a godly trading floor, you sow into the King of Tyre, which means you give that spirit power over your money. Another way we trade with the King of

Tyre is when we say, "I do not have enough," or "I want more." It is not, "I need more," but "I want more! What I have is not sufficient." There is nothing wrong with saying, "Lord, I cannot pay my bills, I need Your help," but when we start looking for avenues to try and empower ourselves to have more money, there can be a driving influence coming from the King of Tyre.

The King of Tyre sacked Jerusalem and took the gold out of the temple. Then he formed the port city of Tyre by the edge of the sea, and Tyre became a trading port – a trading platform based on robbery, and setting a demonic precedent in the supernatural world for trading on the face of the earth.

These demons are after the trading floor of the sons of God, because if they can bring a pollution through idolatrous worship and trading on the seed of the children's children's children, then they can control that trading floor forever. At the top of this little pyramid is the demon called Ethbaal. Then under that is his daughter, Jezebel, which means "Where is Baal?" Jezebel does three things in Israel; she takes charge of the king, she takes charge of the religious system in Israel, and then she starts to kill all the prophets. In the church today we often have a Jezebel spirit that rules, governs and controls the religious concepts and systems and kills the prophets. Every time we use coercion to take up an offering or manipulate people to do something, it is witchcraft, and trading on Jezebel's trading floor.

"The word of the LORD came to me again, saying, "Son of man, say to the prince of Tyre, 'Thus says the Lord GOD: "Because your heart is lifted up, And you say, 'I am a god, I sit in the seat of gods, In the midst of the seas,' Yet you are a man, and not a god, Though you set your heart as the heart of a god Behold, you are wiser than Daniel! There is no secret that can be hidden from you!" (Ezekiel 28:1-3).

There is a principle here. The Roman Catholics have a seat for the Pontiff. When he sits in that seat he is speaking as God, because when you sit as a son in a seat of government you can speak as a prince or as a king, and you speak as a godlike one. *"Jesus answered them, "Is it not written in your Law, 'I SAID, YOU ARE GODS [human judges representing God, not divine beings]'?"* (John 10:34 AMP). On the right trading floor that is good. But on a wrong trading floor, you are trading right into a demonic kingdom. The Prince of Tyre was seen as god and he called himself god. That also happened in Paul's day, *"Herod, arrayed in royal apparel, sat on his throne and gave an oration to them. And the people kept shouting, "The voice of a god and not of a man!" Then immediately an angel of the Lord struck him, because he did not give glory to God. And he was eaten by worms and died"* (Acts 12:21-23). The same demon spirit is still operating today.

"With your wisdom and your understanding You have gained riches for yourself, And gathered gold and silver into your treasuries; By your great wisdom in trade you have increased your riches, And your heart is lifted up because of your riches)," (Ezekiel 28:4-5).

The riches come from trading, so my heart has been lifted up because of my abilities to trade to gain for myself. Whoever has the gold has the glory. That is why the church does not have the gold. It is because the demonic spirit world knows the silver and the gold belong to the children of YHVH. If they have it they have the glory. The demonic world gains it by a false trading floor. The heavens belong to the highest bidder. How much are you trading?

"Therefore thus says the Lord GOD: "Because you have set your heart as the heart of a god, Behold, therefore, I will bring strangers against you, The most terrible of the nations" (Ezekiel 28:6-7).

The terrible nation is us, bringing judgment of the Word of God, which means tearing down the glory of that kingdom to establish another Kingdom.

"...Will you still say before him who slays you, 'I am a god'? But you shall be a man, and not a god In the hand of him who slays you. You shall die the death of the uncircumcised By the hand of aliens; For I have spoken," says the Lord GOD.'" (Ezekiel 28:7, 9-10).

Uncircumcised means *'ones that do not live in covenant relationship'.* Circumcision is all about covenant – the shedding of blood – covenant.

The Hebrew people were circumcised by covenant, which meant they could not give their seed away or spill it unfruitfully. Their seed was given wholly to the purposes and presence of God, uncovered before the presence of the Lord. YHVH says 'circumcise your heart' so that the trading floor of your heart is fully given over to the government of Heaven and you do not spill your seed onto another trading floor.

"...The king of Tyre ... 'Thus says the Lord GOD:"You were the seal of perfection, Full of wisdom and perfect in beauty. You were in Eden, the garden of God; Every precious stone was your covering...

"You were the anointed cherub who covers... I established you; You were on the holy mountain of God; You walked back and forth in the midst of fiery stones. You were perfect in your ways from the day you were created, Till iniquity was found in you.

"By the abundance of your trading You became filled with violence within, And you sinned; Therefore I cast you as a profane thing Out of the mountain of God; And I destroyed you, O covering cherub, From the midst of the fiery stones.

"Your heart was lifted up because of your beauty; You corrupted your wisdom for the sake of your splendor; I cast you to the ground, I laid you before kings, That they might gaze at you. "You defiled your sanctuaries By the multitude of your iniquities, By the iniquity of your trading; Therefore I brought fire from your midst; It devoured you, And I turned you to ashes upon the earth In the sight of all who saw you. All who knew you among the peoples are astonished at you; You have become a horror, And shall be no more forever" (Ezekiel 28:12-19).

Iniquity can be described as *'whatever the eye hooks into, multiplies'*. Satan saw opportunity, hooked into it, and it began to multiply in him. We are the kings the Word is talking about here. Satan is going to be laid before us, and we will be revealed to him as kings. Our pleasure with brass feet is that we smash his head (Revelation 2:18).

The demonic is totally and absolutely vulnerable to you and me with no answer for anything, when we stand and start trading in the right way as a king in our own mountain and in the mountain of YHVH – in the Kingdom of God inside of us, and in the Kingdom of Heaven, which is on the outside of us. When you and I trade on both we get the Kingdom of God and the Kingdom of Heaven joined together – power! The Father allowed the Lamb to be crucified at the very beginning of the foundations of the world (Revelation 13:8). He was looking all the way down to the year 00000, looking all the way down the generational line to when His

Son was going to be manifested here because He had set up the trade for us there.

Leviathan, Cain and Apollyon

Leviathan is the twister, the perverter, the one that speaks half-truths. So how do we trade with it?

It can be by passing on 'news' through social media:

"Oh, do you know that Ian does this?"

"Have you ever heard him say that?"

"No, but he does it."

"How do you know?"

"Well, somebody said…"

Social media sites can be used as some of the biggest Leviathan trading floors of gossip that man now has on the face of the earth.

Apollyon is the spirit that resists salvation, the one that locks up the seeds of YHVH to stop people coming into the house of God. How do we trade with Apollyon? Every time Jesus has said, "Share the gospel with them; they need to know My grace and salvation," and your heart has faltered so you reasoned it away. You are then trading with the spirit of Apollyon, playing right into its hand. Next time you come to share the gospel, your heart falters and the demon spirit says, "Remember last time you did not share and it did not really matter?", you are trading with the spirit of Apollyon. *"They had as king over them the angel of the bottomless pit, whose name in Hebrew is Abaddon, but in Greek he has the name Apollyon"* (Revelation 9:11).

There are some angelic creatures that operate with each of these demon spirits that are a counterpart to them. The ones that deal with Apollyon are called hunter angels. The Bible tells us in Matthew 22:9 and Luke 14:23 that YHVH sends His servants into the highways and byways and hunts out those to bring to the bridal table. The moment you begin to make a move against Apollyon these hunter angels, as tall as telegraph poles, can take their position because they want to operate with the sons of God to deal with those things.

Jezebel has its basis and roots in witchcraft. Witchcraft is anything to do with manipulation, control or domination. So, wives, do not nag or be a dripping tap. Allow YHVH to do what He has got to do with your husband and speak to him face to face. Husbands love your wives, because if you do not, you are submitting to the spirit of Cain and trading with it. The spirit of Cain murders; if you do not love your wife, you are murdering her. The spirit of Cain is all about murder. Whenever you murder someone in your heart and you speak destructively about them, you are trading on Cain's trading floor. YHVH says do not do these things because He does not want you trading into a system that will destroy your seed's seed.

Cain is one of the worst demon spirit trading floors that the church can ever experience. What did Cain do? *"While they were in the field, Cain rose up against Abel his brother and killed him"* (Genesis 4:8 TLV). Usually those who had the last move of YHVH are the ones who want to murder those that are carrying the new move of YHVH because they do not want to change the way they think. We might think we do not like shaking in church or people who have the freedom to wave flags. Have you ever been into Heaven and seen how weird Heaven is? Everybody is flashing like lightning storms with these amazing colours of vibrant, frenetic ecstacy – welcome to reality!

It is called brotherly love. You are accountable for your attitude towards brother. You are accountable for what goes on inside your heart. If you murder them in your heart, Yeshua said, *"You have heard that it was said, 'You shall not commit adultery.' But I tell you that everyone who looks upon a woman to lust after her has already committed adultery with her in his heart"* (Matthew 5:27-28 TLV). Jesus set a Kingdom principle. So if you murder somebody in your heart you might as well have gone and murdered them. The spirit of Cain operates through the heart of people in church life. It is the worst spirit trading-floor that can operate in church. That is why some pastors leave churches – because they are controlled by a governing board that murders them, trading with the spirit of Cain. The board does not lead the church, the pastor does, as the set leader YHVH put in place to operate positionally, to bring the atmosphere of the glory of God into the church life.

The spirit of Cain operates by the destructive words, actions, deeds, heart issues and thoughts of people in church life against their brothers and sisters. If you will not go and speak to someone personally, but your attitudes and words murder them, then you are trading on Cain's trading floor.

Now it says Jesus took His blood and He cleansed the Heavens when *"He went once for all into the [Holy of] Holies [of heaven], not by virtue of the blood of goats and calves [by which to make reconciliation between God and man], but His own blood, having found and secured a complete redemption (an everlasting release for us)"* (Hebews 9:12 AMP). What did Jesus cleanse the heavens from? He cleansed it from Satan's trading. To make a pathway for you and me to come all the way back to the arc of God and to begin to cover the mercy seat and receive revelation from the presence of the Father, to bring government back into the arena that we lost.

Every time you sacrifice your life you are trading on the sea of glass for something (Revelation 4:6). YHVH calls us, His sons, to come before Him and ask Him for the nations (Psalm 2:8). How do you ask for the nations? You surrender your life and say, "Lord, here I am". The moment you say, "Lord, here I am" you are trading with your life for nations. It is a totally different way of praying.

Our Judicial Bench of Three

One time I was repenting all day. It was weird. But at the end of it, I felt so good, because repentance empowers YHVH to become who He is, which is our judicial committee in the realm of the heavens. This is the Father, the Son and the Holy Spirit, which I call the "bench of three". One of those that comes off the bench of three becomes a court hearer whose name is Jesus. So when you start praying, "I repent Jesus," He says, "I come into agreement with that repentance. It is cleansed".

The devil is sweating, knowing that he is going to get beaten up tomorrow because we are busy repenting today, which means we are going to get revelation on how to destroy the demonic.

YHVH's desire has always been to have someone, a people, or a bride that would trade in righteousness before the throne, out of covenant relationship.

We have a frequency that tabernacles over us. Our thought life and inner life creates an atmosphere through the frequency of the vibration of our thoughts. Our DNA sings a song of our thought life as it sits up over the top of each of us and tabernacles over us.

Other Trading Floors

You can trade anything. I know some people who have traded television and made a choice never to watch television again, praying, "Father, I take this desire to watch television, I come into Your presence, up to the place of Your presence, I step onto the sea of glass and I trade this desire for television. I trade it that I might see into Your Kingdom. I receive that capacity of sight, Father. I descend back from Your presence and I step into this arena here, Father. Thank You that I am going to see as I have traded in faith."

We can trade reading romance magazines or Mills and Boon books. Women can get addicted to the idealised, romanticised image of a man. If we get soul-tied to it, no man will ever fulfil that idealised romanticised image. And so the woman lives soul-tied to a romanticised image of a man that she will never have fulfilment with. When a man fantasises about idealised, erotic images of a woman, when he gets married his wife never fulfils that idealised erotic image inside of him because no one can match up to that faceless thing which is a demon spirit sitting inside his soul that he is soul-tied to. That is why this can cause people trouble – those romantic magazines we read that have all the gossip pages in them or those erotic things that we look at that we do not really want to look at. We need to keep short accounts with them, otherwise it gets your brain in the wrong place and that is Delilah – this is seduction or anything to do with seduction, including religion. Religion seduces you away from the truth to make you believe a lie that your system and your protocols are from Heaven when they are not. It is about a religious system. That is what that Nicaean Council was all about in 320 AD and it wrecked the church.

Delilah will come and trade on your desires. That is why the Bible says, *"Whatever things you ask when you pray, believe that you receive them, and you will have them"* (Mark 11:24). Maybe YHVH is saying you have got wrong things in your heart. It could be something like coveting your neighbour's car, "Man, I covet a Nissan GTR

35". You may have a spirit of Delilah seducing you. The way that seduction works is by empowering you to believe a lie – something that is not true. That is seduction. So you could be trading with Delilah, with Cain on social media, with Athaliah, with Jezebel or with Tyre, by allowing yourself to be seduced into a lie. So you might now be operating with five trading floors on one issue!

Cleaning out your Temple – Sea of Glass

YHVH wants us to be free from this garbage so each of us can function as a son. I have had to clean my house out to prepare my temple and make it so my spirit man is able to be free to receive, to give and to sow.

When you do something to serve the Lord and people say, "Hi, well done, it's really great what you are doing", if you find yourself responding, "Yeah, it is all Jesus," the moment you say, "It is all Jesus," you are rejecting their trading in your life. This means you are trading with Athaliah, who wants to kill the seed of the affirmation you feel unable to receive. I say to people, "Thank you very much. That's awesome, I receive that." They are speaking good things to you. But then in the secret place after I have received it, I pray, "Lord, I come into Your Kingdom realm, up to the place of Your presence, onto the sea of glass. Father, I trade the affirmation of man for Your affirmation of me as a son, and I receive it out of the Kingdom today. I bring it back down here, step into this arena and release it around my life, Father so that I am affirmed as Your son." If you cannot receive it from people, you will never receive it from the Father, because people are YHVH in the flesh speaking to you (1 John 4:20).

YHVH wants us to repent of these things, and my hope is that you recognise and begin to look at where you have traded in your own life. There is a sea of glass where the elders cast their crowns (Revelation 4:6,10). That is a trading floor and what I would do is take back where I have traded. "Father, wherever I have traded with the thought that I might be in full-time ministry by doing this I have traded on the desire right into Jezebel's trading floor. Lord, I repent of that. I take that desire and I lay hold of it and I come into Your presence, up to the place of Your presence, and I lay it on the sea of glass and I trade it for Your desire for me. Lord, I come back down here with Your desire, I step back into this realm and arena, and I release Your desire into the atmosphere of my life."

Every time we have said, "I do not have enough", we have traded with the demon spirit of Tyre. Now you have got to understand I have gone through the ups and downs. But we repented of trading with the Jezebelic trading floor and all the others and made a memorial offering to the Lord. After that a prophetic guy came to the church. When YHVH starts taking notice, first of all the prophets begin to speak it because they are testifying to what you already know is coming to pass.

He said, "Hey, you two over there, I don't know what is going on but there is seven-fold return coming for what you have lost."

And we said "Yes! We will take that!" And we got our seven-fold return.

This is Daddy; out of brokenness you begin to see the salvation of God come. Where you surrender and yield, God's memorial can come and then you trade on His trading floor. Then He can release His name and His Word over your trade and begin to bring increase over it. That is why the elders traded their crowns (Revelation 4:10). They traded their government for higher government so He could bring the increase over their government. It is all about increase. Everything is about increase.

I enjoy talking about Kingdom trading and all the finances that go on in the heavens because I have been there and watched the tables of exchange in Heaven. I know how Heaven's finance operates. I know how the gold comes into the earth. There are things we have got to learn. The Lord has begun to teach me about trading on the sea of glass and the eye of currency trading, and as a king how to dictate to currencies, which is really great.

We are administrators of a higher Kingdom, and a higher order that will bring this earth into divine order. If you administrate out of Heaven the earth will respond to you.

In China there are something like eighty-five million Christians now in the underground ecclesia. The Chinese have been taking more gold out of the ground than America and it is all being done by hand. A lot of it is only six inches under the surface of the land.

This is Daddy doing this. This is what happens when a son stands and begins to speak into the land. After dealing with the dragons and giants you begin to see the release of the Kingdom.

Remember, to be able to engage Heaven you must ascend into the place of the presence of God. There is a difference between going into the realm of the spirit and going into the higher place where you must go, which is into the place of His presence. The place of His presence is where He actually is, not just the fragrance of His presence, which is what we see here. So when we go into the realm of the spirit and we engage the Kingdom, we can step into it. We must ascend into the place of His presence because that is where the trading floor is.

The cross and the blood of Jesus

Just as Jesus traded in divine exchange on the cross so that we would benefit, the cross of Christ is the first place we trade, losing our garbage and trading for His glory. The cross of Jesus Christ has got to be real in your life. I went through a situation having to face the cross of Christ in my life. A situation happened and because I am prophetic, I was able to go back in time and go into the meeting where they were talking about me and a whole lot of things were said about my life that were not right.

I decided to challenge those people, to get in their faces and deal with the demonic stuff that they were operating in. So I went to make an appointment to talk with these two guys face-to-face. But that appointment never happened so I was starting to get mad because I knew what went on. And yet, whenever I see them they are still saying, "Hi, Brother Ian" and shaking my hand, "Hi, Brother Ian great to see you today! It is wonderful how YHVH is moving."

I wanted to say to them, "But you said these things about me, so what is all this? You are trading on a demonic trading floor, buddy. I can see into your life and I see the demons speaking to me. Having to go through the motions whenever I saw them, "Hi, Brother Ian, great to see you today,"

I would think, 'Huh, huh, but that is not what is going on in your heart. I can see your heart and what is going on inside your life'.

I was busy praying one morning and beginning to decree the

Word of God that it would stand over me, and I was learning about some things in the realm of the Kingdom. Then the Lord said to me, "Son, I love you."

I said, "Yes Lord. I know You do."

He said, "I love Jesus as well."

"Yes Lord, I know you did because you sent Him," and we had this wonderful conversation, until the Lord said, "You know, He stood before Pilate and was accused and said nothing. Are you prepared to say nothing?"

I said, "Yes Lord, I will say nothing. I will be the good Christian and say nothing." And that was it.

But as I came out of my prayer time, the demonic arguments rushed in, "Ian, you need to justify yourself. You need to get in their face and tell them."

"But the Lord said… "

"Ian, you need to justify yourself. Ian, they treat you like dirt. They disrespect who you are."

"Yeah, but He said…"

"They really disrespect who you are." And a week went past with this demon whispering this into my ear.

Each time I thought, 'I am going to…'

YHVH said, "Are you prepared to die?"

I said, "Yes", so it meant I needed to walk to the cross and begin to trade with the cross here.

So when this thing would come whispering in my ear, I would say, "Father, I nail this thing to the cross in the Name of Jesus. I take its power and its voice. It is a liar. It decrees the things that are not born out of the voice and the heart of YHVH. I crucify you on the cross." I thought when I did that once it would stop. But no – it happened seven hundred times a day! "Father, I take this thing in the Name of Jesus I bind you". Week after week after week after week – six months into it I was still in the middle of this horrendous war with dunghill heaped all around me, sitting on my donkey asking, "Oh Lord, what is this? I am supposed to die at the cross – it is supposed to flee from me." Then the Lord said, "You are carrying your cross," and He asked me, "Why do you go to the cross?"

I said, "Lord, to deal with all my garbage."

"Yeah, but why do you go?"

I said, "Well Lord, to hang it there."

He repeated the question, "Yeah, but why do you go?"

"Well Lord, I do not know. You know. I need You to tell me."

Then He said, "To go through it, because what is on the other side is the freedom. And so you have got to use your experience as a springboard to engage the cross and go beyond it to the freedom."

Now my whole life began to change. Instead of waiting for those things to come so I could fight them, I was waiting and welcoming them to come to springboard me into relationship with the Father. So they would come and whisper in my ear and I would go 'whack' and suddenly I was in the spirit realm. Now throughout the day I was starting to walk in the spirit because this thing would whisper in my ear to engage me, which would spring-board me into the presence of God. I spent a year trading my sin at the cross of Christ, trading the whispers of the demons at His cross, taking my life, dying to it and trading for His life on the other side to receive internal life. That thing will never have another anchor in my life because I want intimacy with the Father more than I want that thing speaking to me.

At the end of that year I had an encounter with YHVH in the dark cloud where I saw, for the first time the Person of YHVH face to face (see the chapter "The Dark Cloud" in Realms of the Kingdom Volume 1). I spoke with the Person of YHVH.

The first time I saw Him I could not lift my eyes up because all my religious theology said, "If I see YHVH I am going to die", but boy, I wanted to look. It took me four times going there before I looked. When I did look it was, "Wow! Look at that. I am going into eternity, but look at that face changing." It was wonderful, but the first time I saw Him He was crying. There were these tears dripping on the floor.

In my heart I said, "Lord, what is going on? Why are You crying?"

He said to me, "Son, it has been a long time since anybody has been here."

I tell you it broke my heart. That is how much YHVH has

desired relationship with the sons of men and we have not chased Him. The cross is an important trading floor for us.

The blood of Christ

We need to engage the blood of Christ and at the end of this chapter we are going to have communion, and we will follow through in trading on this important trading floor of divine exchange.

When people drop money into baskets around conference halls they are trading into revelation. This is a heavenly trading floor. Trading into revelation is a good thing because you give according to what YHVH has laid on your heart, not what you have been manipulated to feel guilty about. Every time you sow out of guilt or manipulation and give out of a religious system, it is about control. So you give 10% every week thinking, "I have given my 10%, I expect YHVH to give me back!" That is trading into a religious system, which brings you under control. So you are giving your money to Jezebel's trading floor.

Terumah and tithing are Old Testament principles. Giving and offerings are New Testament principles that mean more than the original. We give 10% and think we are doing well. "I gave 10% this week." Well no wonder you are not being blessed, because you are not giving terumah and more.

The blood of Christ needs to be applied to every aspect of your life. It is a place of exchange where you exchange your DNA for His. The blood of Jesus is not just the nip and the sip of a cup on a Sunday morning. It is about the record of the DNA of the Son of God that was given to the face of the earth. YHVH gave His DNA to the earth so that you and I could become sons born of His DNA. That is why the Bible says in 1 John, *"No one who has been born from God practices sin, because God's seed abides in him"* (1 John 3:9 ISV). Your DNA has been converted to the true DNA of YHVH your Father. It says, *"...Anyone born of God does not keep on sinning... and the evil one cannot touch him"* (1 John 5:18 TLV). So if you find yourself being hit or slimed by demons it is because you have not got enough of the blood of Jesus. You need to start taking communion more than once a week or once a month – two or three times a day – engaging the reality of the transference of the resonance of the DNA and the frequency and record of who YHVH is into your body, so your body can digest it and take on the image of that record. That is why we have communion; it is a very powerful trading floor.

The crown of thorns that Jesus wore is another trading floor. You have your own trading floors in your heart and your mountain and you have got to deal with all these things. Nehemiah 13 talks about the priestly room for storing the wine, corn and oil, which is all about abundance, that was given to Tobiah, which was so wrong because he was a Gentile using it unlawfully.

YHVH wants us to rule on the mountains. The Bible says,

"Now it shall come to pass in the latter days That the mountain of the LORD's house Shall be established on the top of the mountains, And shall be exalted above the hills; And all nations shall flow to it" (Isaiah 2:2).

YHVH wants to manifest the glory of the mountain of His throne up here on every single one of these mountains, to bring proper government into what was, what is, and what is to come. YHVH wants the ecclesia to come into the reality of what it means to trade in the heavens.

Trading on the Sea of Glass

Trading in the heavens takes practice; you may not feel anything but that does not mean to say nothing has happened; it just means you have not caught up with the fact that you have done something – it requires faith. It may seem like a weird thing to go up into His presence, go onto the sea of glass and trade, then come back down here, step out and release it. But you are learning a pathway of entry into the realm of Heaven. The more you practice the pathway, the faster you can go. So you can ascend and descend. That is why the Bible says, *"Angels of God ascending and descending upon the Son of Man"* (John 1:51). You can go up and down. The more you learn the pathway the quicker you can do it, the more you can trade, the easier it is to trade and the faster you can trade. There are times when I specifically slow everything down because I want to enjoy the journey. But there are times when you do not have time to enjoy the journey, you have just got to trade.

Sometimes when I cannot mow the lawns I sit at my computer

and pretend I am at my computer. The issue is I am trading up and down – communicating and engaging the Kingdom, walking in the spirit, seeing things, going there, standing on the sea of glass and sinking into it. One of the times I turned up on the sea of glass and I sank into it, because you are a trade yourself. You trade yourself as a living sacrifice that the glory would flow through your life into the world that is around you. So I stood on the sea of glass and I traded myself. All that was left behind was just a few stones. I prayed, "Lord, that is not much to trade with, is it really?"

I am trading as a living stone so I left my stone there because I want to become a pillar (Revelation 3:12) not just a stone. So I traded, "Lord, this little stone for a pillar". Then I realised, 'Wait a minute, in Eden, in the river there are many stones. I wonder if I can get some of those, stick them in my belly and take them on the sea of glass?' So I went into Eden, walked on the river and took some stones. Because the more you get the better you feel. So I took this big belly full to trade and came back up into the place of His presence and went onto the sea of glass. "Lord, I'm trading stones of Heaven!" That is what they are there for. Just go and do it, it is fun!

Activation

Please get some bread and wine or juice for yourself.

I would like to present an offering. If you do not have any money to give I would ask you to borrow a coin from somebody. I would really like you to have something because I want to trade with your offering. As you take communion I want us to trade.

When you put your offering in, do not just throw it in – allow your heart to feel.

Father, with what I have here I am trading into the revelations I have received; I am trading into the heavens for our nation; I am trading for the glory of God to fill our nation here.

Father, today we have come into agreement with Your Word, which says that if I eat this body and drink this blood I am going to live forever. Father, we come into agreement with Your Word that this is the record of YHVH and that as I eat it and drink it I am partaking of the Father who is in Heaven. Lord, today I acknowledge that, as this goes into my body, the resurrection life and the ability to live forever and to be raised in this last day in resurrection power is going into my body. I will receive the record in my DNA of this, Your DNA. The divine exchange will occur inside of my life with this glory that I now hold in my hand.

Father, today I eat freely, willingly and with full knowledge of what I am doing, looking to the author and finisher of my faith, that in this there is everlasting life.

I want you to hold the communion up in the air now.

Lord, in this there is a sacrifice and an offering and we present Your body on the sea of glass. Father, today we trade in the heavens with the blood and body of Jesus Christ. We trade in the heavens for our nation in the name of Jesus.

Father, we want to lift the finances that have been given. Father, we take them with the blood and body of Jesus onto the sea of glass and we buy a nation with what we have given – in the blood and body of Jesus, in the finances that we have given and of our time. Father, we buy a nation in the realm of the spirit tonight in the name of Jesus. Father, we offer it up as a trade in the heavens; we offer it up as a trade of what You have given us. We offer it up to buy silver and gold for this nation.

Lord, as we eat and we drink, we drink the power of eternal life. Lord, we receive it in our bodies today. As we eat I ask that the glory of eternal life would flood my being and penetrate into the atmosphere around me right now in the name of Jesus Christ.

Let's eat.

Let's stand and begin to pray in the spirit. I want you to get your spirit man wrapped around this revelation that we each now have in our bellies the blood and the body of Jesus that brings life to us as spirit beings.

Father, I reach in and I brood over the record that is now in my body. I brood over it today and I call forth the life that is within it. I call forth all the power of the resurrection life. In the name of Jesus Christ I call forth all the healing power that is in that body. Father, I ask You to bless my body as it digests this substance, that the record will penetrate into my DNA so that I would be changed into Your image from glory to glory.

Father, today we reach into the realm of Your Kingdom and we draw the abundance of the house of wine around our lives to testify of the abandonment to Your glory and to Your presence. Father, I receive out of the Kingdom realm. Father, I ask that the chancellors would bring the wine bottles out of all that we need to drink and this record would come around our lives, that we would drink and drink and drink until the record becomes satisfied inside of us, in the name of Jesus.

Father, let the saints of old testify, let the angels of YHVH witness and testify. Father, let the seven Spirits of God witness and testify in the name of Jesus. Amen.

CHAPTER 10

UNDERSTANDING ANGELS

YHVH is releasing knowledge of the angelic, mystical realm of the spirit world onto the face of the earth today. We can engage, cooperate with and become a part of this realm. You are not just by yourself doing the work, preaching the Word or taking the gospel out into the highways and byways. When you move there are angels that move with you.

There are many different stations and protocols of angels. Some just come with messages and they will speak; some are guiding and they watch over you; some are assigned to your testimony scroll from when you were in the realm of eternity because you came out of the realm of eternity with angels assigned to your life.

Angels are really interesting beings. My first encounter with an angel was over 25 years ago. I did not really know about the angelic world because nobody would teach about it. Speaking into the spirit world, something I used to pray was, "Father I thank You for Your Word that is sharper than any two edged sword. Father, as Your Word says – it is finished, I speak into the spirit world – it is finished!" When I pray like that my spirit is praying, because I learned how to pray in tongues in English so I did not have to think about what I was praying. I could think about something else in my brain while I was praying out of my mouth, but I can still understand what I am saying while my brain is having another whole conversation all on its own. I was busy praying and wondering what it actually does in the spirit world when I pray, "It is finished!" How does this work? What does the Word do?

We used to play with swords when we were young, so I was

thinking about the Word of God and a sword and what it was like when I slipped into the spirit realm. This was my first transition into the Kingdom world as a believer. As it opened up I was standing next to an angel that was as tall as a telegraph pole. I thought, 'What do I do?!' No one ever talks about angels and now there is this really scary thing looking at me! I was stunned looking up at it. It took the sword from its side and when it drew its sword, the sword was probably about eight feet long judging from the angel's height. It drew what looked like a small sword out of its side and said to me, "Hear what the Spirit of the Lord is saying to the church today." Then it took that sword and went to swipe it in the spirit world and I saw, "Father it is finished" written on the sword. Our decrees empower the angels to carry the Word of God forth to change the atmosphere. So I said, "Father it is finished" and it struck the sword into the spirit world. When its arms were almost horizontal the sword started to stretch right out as far as I could see until I could not see the end of the sword. Then the angel put the sword back into its side and smiled down at me. I was freaking out but then I suddenly found myself back at home. We may not always engage angels in the smooth way we imagine we would because angels are supernatural beings, but after a while you get used to being around the magnificence of their presence.

I had been busy praying and trying to deal with something inside my life, and one day I was in a meeting. The prayer ministry team were quietly going round just standing there praying in tongues and then going on to pray with the next person during our time with Holy Spirit. Then someone came and stood next to me, put their hands on me and started to pray. I was thinking, 'Wow this person is so sensitive', because I am this spiritual freak that nobody wants to come and pray with because they manifest if they have got devils in them. People usually left me alone and prayed for everyone else except me. But someone was laying hands on me in this meeting and I continued thinking, 'Wow, this is amazing' for half an hour. I had never been ministered to by an angel before. So by the time they came to the end of the session, waiting in the presence of God, I turned around to thank them for praying for me and there was no one there but the hand was still on my shoulder. Then my eyes opened in the spirit realm and I saw this angel looking at me. Once you get used to being around the angelic world then it is not such a hard thing.

When angels show up it is not the intense presence of God that they bring. There is a fluffy, light, happy, nice, yummy, warm, fuzzy feeling. It is different from the presence of Jesus or the presence of Holy Spirit when He comes into a room. The atmosphere changes because we create a platform. The more you speak about the angelic, the more they want to come and see the vibration that sounds like them and sit into it. So that is why I love talking about the angelic world, because it unlocks that whole realm and arena for us to engage.

We were in Los Angeles one springtime and I had just finished teaching on the angelic canopy there. The atmosphere in the room became electric. As we came to have the next meeting and we started to worship, I was on the left hand side of the church so that I could watch what was going on and then I saw the sound guy step back, a bit freaked out, looking at his sound desk because the volume knobs were starting to move. The sound was getting better and better as the volume knobs moved. He was freaking out because he was not doing it! He gestured to the musicians and the guy playing the piano took his hands completely away but the piano was still playing, and it was playing better music than he had been playing! Everybody started seeing this, all asking, "Umm… what's going on here?!" Then the room went "crack" as the spirit realm opened up and there were hundreds of angels just waiting to minister to the people who had never experienced angelic ministry to them as individuals before. So we spent the next half an hour with people being ministered to inside the meeting by angels of the Lord who are sent on assignment.

Hunter Angels

Another time when I was overseas, as we were praying into the nation, we went to stand on the sea shore. About 120 miles from the shore there was a spiritual gateway that the demonic world had used to birth stuff into that nation, which then birthed it into the whole continent. As a group of people we went after the gate because whoever holds the gates holds the entry to the city.

We began to pray and intercede there, going into the realm of the Kingdom to engage the demonic realm that sat in that gate. The Lord gave us words about this demon called Apollyon that controlled the gateway. So we began to engage in warfare with this demonic spirit of Apollyon. When you are in the realm of the Kingdom there are things that happen around you, and sometimes you are distracted, focusing on the natural world, hoping something would happen, instead of being in the Kingdom world, which is where we are supposed to function from, to administrate on the earth. We were in the spirit world, in the Kingdom realm, beginning to administrate the desire of YHVH on the face of the earth, to bring revival into that nation. The spirit of Apollyon is the thing that resists the souls of men and women coming into salvation. It is the thing that stops salvation flowing because it is of a different seed from the seed of the sons of God.

As we began to pray, this spirit started to rise up out of the sea. It was amazing to watch this happen. I said to our group, "Take a step forward" and as we took a step forward there was a massive bending and shifting of the spirit realm that was around us. When we looked to the right and to the left of us there were angels about 20 feet high just spread right along the shore as far as we could see. I was fascinated and had suddenly forgotten all about what we were doing. I was going, "Wowwwww!" It was one of those moments when things changed for us as we realised that we were not alone as a group of people standing there doing something.

I am curious about those kinds of mysterious things and I wanted to know how they function, why they are there, how they turned up, why they turned up and what they do because of what I am doing. So I took another step forward. When I took another step forward, the whole rank went forwards. So I took a step backwards; and the whole lot took a step backwards. So I started going forwards and backwards. I was being really naughty, but I wanted to understand. When you find a new toy you play with it, until you realise how serious the toy really is. Well I am like a kid when the realm of the Kingdom begins to open up. I want to know how it works. So I was busy praying with all these people and they could see what was happening. They were all saying, "Wow! Did you see that?" I could feel the shaking, in the natural realm, from the noise of the ranks of angels moving. As we stood there I began to pray, "Father, thank You that this gateway belongs to us!" And I heard, "Yep, yep, yep, yep, yep..." on either side.

We mandate angels to do their job, so as we move they come into agreement. That is an important issue. But unless you are doing what you are supposed to be doing, they will not be working with you. You have got to do what you are supposed to be doing, which is advancing the Kingdom, or else you will end up doing it by yourself, which is why you get beaten up when the spirit world smacks you.

I thought, 'Well Lord, I am going to take a step'. So I took another step out and thought, 'Lord this time I am going to step outside this natural world and step right into the Kingdom realm because I can see it and I want to be right there with them.'

In the Bible, John says, *"I looked, and behold, a door standing open in heaven. And the first voice which I heard was like a trumpet speaking with me, saying, "Come up here, and I will show you things which must take place after this." Immediately I was in the Spirit..."* (Revelation 4:1-2).

So I thought, if I was going to be in the spirit, I would go by faith, so I stepped in. It did not really change much, except that it was not water any more – it was accessible. For me, as we began to move towards this thing, the whole angelic rank and file began to move towards me.

The demonic world often portrays stuff around us and gives us imagery through films and media. 'The Exorcist' is a film that portrays demons as being very powerful. As a believer, you have more glory, dominion and power than the biggest demonic spirit could ever have. When you turn up, they have to move out, because the battle is already won in Christ. The biggest issue is our turning up. If you do not turn up then you do not win and the angels do not win. Angels are bored because we are not doing our job.

Then I took another step forward, and I shouted, "Yeah!" As I began to shout, it opened a door – I did not have to go into it, the ranks of angels all went into it. I said, "Lord, give me a Scripture for this". There is a Scripture that refers to angels called 'hunter angels'. *"Then the master said to the servant, 'Go out into the highways and hedges, and compel them to come in, that my house may be filled"* (Luke 14:23). They are called hunter angels and they are 20 feet high, they are not little tiddly-winky beings. They are bigger than us, as wide as half a building and there are just ranks of them. As we began to move and to shout into the gate to make it our possession and take our rightful place in that gate, that whole angelic host went inside there and cleaned it out. By this stage I was fascinated, thinking, 'Oh my gosh. I wonder what is not happening on the face of the earth because we are not doing what we are supposed to be doing'. With the angelic realm standing around, leaning on their swords yawning and saying "Boy, this is a boring day today, there are no believers standing up, hallelujah.'" So, I went through this process of looking at some studies of angels.

Angelology

The basis of demonology is 'angelology'. Since demons come from fallen angels, we must have an understanding of what angels are to really understand what demons are. Our biggest problem is that you can go into any Christian bookshop and buy hundreds of books on demons, but you cannot buy any studies on angels. And so our real issue is that we do not really know what the demons are and how to deal with them, because we do not really know what angels are.

The word "angel" comes from the Greek word angelos, which means "a messenger, or an agent of change". The name, Los Angeles means "The Angels". The demon that rules over there is a lost Angel. The Hebrew word for angel is 'malak'. When you look at the word malak, it means the same thing but it also means coming out of Heaven as an ambassador for another Kingdom. But these ambassadorial administrators cannot appropriate their assignments if the sons of God are not operating in what has already been given to them to appropriate. So angels cannot bring the ambassadorial rights in the realm that YHVH has empowered them to release on the face of the earth when we are not doing our part. The Lord wants us to do our part so that they can be released to do their part.

Jesus said, *"Do you think that I cannot now pray to My Father, and He will provide Me with more than twelve legions of angels?"* (Matthew 26:53). Do you realise how many angels are in twelve legions? That is 70,000! The issue is that even one could prevail. In the Bible a single angel is recorded as killing over 180,000 men in one evening: "That night the angel [messenger] of the LORD went out and killed one hundred eighty-five thousand men in the Assyrian camp. When the people got up early the next morning, they saw all the dead bodies" (2 Kings 19:35 EXB).

There are 70,000 angels that you and I have assigned to our life – as it is in God. Jesus said, *"In that day, you will know that I am in My Father, you are in Me, and I am in you"* (John 14:20 TLV). This means that as I am in the Father, I take on the same semblance of Christ. That means everything Jesus had at his disposal is now at our disposal, *"Then I looked, and I heard the voice of many angels around the throne, the living creatures, and the elders; and the number of them was ten thousand times ten thousand, and thousands of thousands"* (Revelation 5:11).

"And Yeshua came up to them and spoke to them, saying, "All authority in heaven and on earth has been given to Me. Go therefore..." (Matthew 28:18-19 TLV). Yeshua HaMashia gave that endowment of power and authority to you and me. Which means everything Jesus did we can do, and everything that was at Jesus' disposal is at our disposal. So welcome to a tabernacling tent of 70,000 angels over your life – personally available for you at any given point, wherever you choose to engage them. The issue is we need to choose to engage them.

It is amazing what can be uncovered inside your Bible. This is the Kingdom of God that young people are going to grow up with, whether we like it, believe it, understand it, or do not receive it – our doctrines are immaterial. It is in the Bible; it is available to you and me. This is the Kingdom that the Father wants to release into our lives to empower us to take the land where the enemy has held ground against us. Whether you do it or do not do it, I am going to – if you will not use your 70,000 and they get bored being around you, I will happily use them and I am quite happy to have them as my portion. This is not just for young people, but those passionate for the Lord. I am young but I am old. It is called living in the realm of eternity today. That is why Caleb said at the age of eighty *"I am as strong this day as on the day that Moses sent me; just as my strength was then, so now is my strength for war, both for going out and for coming in. Now therefore, give me this mountain of which the LORD spoke in that day; for you heard in that day how the Anakim were there, and that the cities were great and fortified. It may be that the LORD will be with me, and I shall be able to drive them out as the LORD said!"* (Joshua 14:11-12). Joshua did not go after the plains or the easy places, he went after the mountains because the giants were there, and whoever gets the giants gets the prize.

Angels are not all the same. Can you imagine if everyone you met said, "Hello human being. Hello human being. Hello human being." There would be no individuality. But we greet each other with different names, which brings an individual basis of encounter. So you do not just say, "Angels come", you go and find out what their names are. It is about developing relationship. The Bible has many people talking with angels, and also talking with the Cloud of Witnesses.

Angels Have a Sense of Humour
Angels are very interesting beings. One of my first encounters was when I was in a church preaching. I was only just getting to know the angelic realm and its function. I did not realise angels have a sense of humour. Angels are not always serious, they do find things funny. "The one who sits in heaven [God] laughs…" (Psalm 2:4 EXB). We think we are funny when we are drunk in the Holy Spirit. When Father goes into His house of wine and He gets drunk on the joy of what He sees His Son doing, He laughs – roaring belly laughs! Angels were made in His signature and likeness; they carry His glory and His desire, therefore they are going to laugh at things too.

An early encounter with an angel taught me that they have a sense of humour. I was in a church preaching from the pulpit when my inner eye (the eye of my spirit man) started to take over my natural eyes and I started seeing from the inside out. I saw an angel in the middle of the church on the great big rafter beam across the centre of the church. This angel was swinging round the rafter beam, upside down, swinging around, looking at me like they do in gymnastics. The angel was going around and around this beam and it would stop upside down, look at me and say, "Go, Ian! Go Ian! Go, Ian!" My family were sitting in the front row. They could see something was going on and I was thinking, 'Oh my gosh, how can I preach with this going on?!' I turned sideways but here is the problem: when you are in the Kingdom realm you see around 360 degrees, but I did not understand that at this stage. So you can turn this way, but you can still see that way. Your spirit man will look wherever the activity is. That is one of those things you learn after a while. So I was turning away but still seeing it and thinking, 'Oh no!'

YHVH was beginning to teach me that it is okay to interact with the angelic realm. I want to know why they are there, what their purpose is, what their function is, what their name is, what their mandate is, what their authorisation is and what their empowerment is. I want to know what they are there for. The only way you can find out what they are there for is to say, "Hi! Why are you here? What is your name? What is your function?" Their name will speak of their function anyway. It builds a bit of relationship, and it is important for that to happen for us.

Angels Ministering to God's People in the Bible

Understanding the angelic realm and what angels are is one of the most important things for us. In both the Old and the New Testament there are instances of angels ministering to God's people.

An angel brought a message to Hagar in the wilderness, *"Hagar fled... But the Angel of the LORD found her by a spring of water in the wilderness, on the road to [Egypt by way of] Shur"* (Genesis 16:6-7 AMP).

An angel brought food to Elijah, "Then he lay down under the broom tree and went to sleep. Suddenly, an angel touched him and said to him, "Get up and eat!" He looked, and there by his head was a cake baked on the hot stones and a jug of water. He ate and drank, then lay down again. The angel came again, a second time, touched him and said, "Get up and eat, or the journey will be too much for you" (1 Kings 19:5-7 CJB).

An angel protected Daniel in the lion's den, *"My God sent His angel and shut the lions' mouths, so that they have not hurt me, because I was found innocent before Him"* (Daniel 6:22).

An angel met Moses in the wilderness, *"Now Moses was tending the flock... And the Angel of the LORD appeared to him in a flame of fire from the midst of a bush..."* (Exodus 3:1-2).

An angel brought the father of John the Baptist the message of John's conception and call, *"Then an angel of the Lord appeared to him... when Zacharias saw him, he was troubled, and fear fell upon him. But the angel said to him, "Do not be afraid, Zacharias, for your prayer is heard; and your wife Elizabeth will bear you a son, and you shall call his name John"* (Luke 1:11-13).

An angel brought the gift of God's healing, *"An angel went down at a certain time into the pool and stirred up the water; then whoever stepped in first, after the stirring of the water, was made well of whatever disease he had"* (John 5:4).

An angel supernaturally released Peter from prison, *"Now behold, an **angel** of the Lord stood by him, and a light shone in the prison; and he struck Peter on the side and raised him up, saying, "Arise quickly!" And his chains fell off his hands"* (Acts 12:7).

Yeshua himself spoke of angels who ministered for Him. *"The Son of Man will send out His angels, and they will gather out of His kingdom all things that offend, and those who practice lawlessness, and will cast them into the furnace of fire. There will be wailing and gnashing of teeth"* (Matthew 13:41-42).

"And He said to him, "Most assuredly, I say to you, hereafter you shall see heaven open, and the angels of God ascending and descending upon the Son of Man" (John 1:51).

Our sonship brings us into the company of angels, *"But you have come to Mount Zion and to the city of the living God, the heavenly Jerusalem, to an innumerable company of angels"* (Hebrews 12:22).

"Relief to you who suffer trouble along with us. At the revelation of the Lord Yeshua from heaven with His mighty angels in flaming fire..." (2 Thessalonians 1:7 TLV).

Angels are *"ministering spirits sent forth to minister for those who will inherit salvation"* (Hebrews 1:14). That means you and me.

The elect angels, those that have not fallen and are still around the throne of YHVH, are worshippers. That worship is solely directed by the revelation of the throne of YHVH. They never seek the worship of man. Only fallen angels desire the worship of man. So if you encounter any angel that says, "You need to bow down to me" it is not an angel of YHVH, it is an emissary out of Hell, because angels are there to serve you as a son, not for you to bow down to them. Angels are terrified of the sons of God because the Bible says, *"Do you not know that we shall judge angels?"* (1 Corinthians 6:3).

Scripture says angels desire to look into the things that are purposed and destined for the sons of God (1 Peter 1:12). They want to look into the things that have been purposed for your life. They wait for you to do your stuff so they can do their stuff because they know what is on the scroll of your testimony. They were there watching it when it came out of the realm of eternity. They have a witness of what has gone on there; they know what was released out of there and they want to see it fulfilled here because they are assigned to its fulfilment. The moment you start to unwrap your scroll and begin to engage who you are and the testimony of what you carry inside of you, as a mandate out of the realm of eternity – when you come into agreement with that it forms an arc of light between Heaven and earth, and then as it is in Heaven, so it is on the earth. And they begin to get motivated and mandated because in Heaven it is already fulfilled and so, on the earth you can begin to walk in it.

Do you realise that two DNA cells can be taken from one person and one can be sent many miles away from the other cell and still register a reaction to the stimulus given to the other one? A study was done where they separated two cells, taking one 149 miles away from the other one. Then they put a sound frequency over the bit of DNA in the original location. The other bit of DNA that was 149 miles away began to vibrate at the same frequency as the original cell without any known connection. This is what happens when we begin to engage the realm of the Kingdom where the Father is. It releases power that is full of angels' provision and full of angelic ministry, full of angelic administration and full of angels who want to come around you and minister.

I sometimes say, "Ministering angels come and minister to me. I welcome your administration of restoration to me to restore my voice, restore my body and empower me to walk in His presence." Then my voice starts to feel a lot better because there are angels that are available and the moment we begin to open up to the presence of God, they will begin to administrate around our life. The Bible says that angels came and ministered to Jesus while He was in the garden (Luke 22:43). You have got to welcome them. People have told me that it is just familiar spirits but it is not. Familiar spirits demand your allegiance to sin. Familiar spirits are those little things that sit on your shoulder and say, "Come and do this thing now, it does not really matter. No one really knows". Familiar spirits are little things that speak in the first person inside your mind. They are demons that desire your allegiance to sin to empower them. On the sacrifice of your sin you mandate them to have authority over your life!

Angels are different. They are, *"ministering spirits sent forth to minister for those who will inherit salvation"* (Hebrews 1:14). The Bible says, *"He Who makes His angels spirits,*

His ministers a flame of fire" (Psalm 104:4).

Angels are worshippers, *"All the angels stood around the throne and the elders and the four living creatures, and fell on their faces before the throne and worshiped God"* (Revelation 7:11).

Angels are extremely obedient to the desire of YHVH and they are unquestionably perfect in their obedience to the commands of YHVH –

"Bless the LORD, you His angels,
You mighty ones who do His commandments,
Obeying the voice of His word!" (Psalm 103:20 AMP).

Angels are Very Wise

"...Like the wisdom of the angel of God, to know everything that is in the earth" (2 Samuel 14:20 AMP).

The angels' wisdom has increased over the ages. They are very wise, although they do not have the great wisdom of YHVH in them. They also do not have the wisdom of YHVH that has been given to us as sons. As we mature in the things of YHVH, they get wiser about their role in YHVH, because they have been assigned to the spirit of a person from where they were released from out of the realm of eternity. You and I came out the realm of eternity as spirit beings. You and I are not human beings, we are spirit beings that have a soul that live in a physical body.

Angels long to look into the secrets that YHVH has put in us because what we carry they do not carry and they are fascinated that the God of the universe chose to take a bit of Himself and put it into a physical body called a human being. They look at that and go, "Whoa!" They are busy looking at YHVH in the life of a person. The more you open up, the more they can see. When you start talking about revelation and the things that are coming, the angelic world begins to get mobilised. They are very interested in what you have to say because you are the one who is going to be the mouthpiece of YHVH's revelation on the earth out of your relationship with Him and be able to speak life into the world that they can function into.

The angelic realm is as close to you as the air that you breathe. The Father wants the angelic realm to be activated around your life so that you are never alone. Suddenly the spirit world becomes very real when you thought it was not very real, and your salvation is real when you really did not think it was really real, because there is a spirit realm as close to you as the air that you breathe. And when you turn into it, it becomes the source of your supply. Angels are that close to us. Some of them are sitting right with us.

The Character of Angels

Only fallen angels rise up in pride requiring us to serve them, and they will bring terror with them to judge and to make you afraid, to try to stand over the top of you. That is a demon, not an angel. The elect angels bear meekness and gentleness and carry the character of YHVH. *"Yet Michael the archangel, in contending with the devil, when he disputed about the body of Moses, dared not bring against him a reviling accusation, but said, "The Lord rebuke you!"* (Jude 9). An angel recognises who you are, and what you are to the person and presence of God, and that you are a son. Therefore you are of great value to them because you are of great value to the Father.

They do the bidding of the Father and if they do the Father's bidding and we are sons of the Father's house, they will do our bidding as well. But I do not say, "Hey you! Go and fetch me a cup of coffee". That is not what they are there for. They are there to serve the mandate of the authorisation of YHVH in you as the presence of God manifests out of you, through you and around you into the world. Angels can begin to occupy the essence of YHVH that is displayed around your life. That is why we have got to walk in the light, because the greater the light that is around you, the greater the measure of the appearance of the angelic world around you, the greater the demonic world will back off from you. The more we spend time in the light, the greater the manifestation of YHVH inside you because when you are in the light, all your junk gets opened and gets seen so you can deal with it. The reason we do not always want to be in the light is because sometimes we want our junk and we like it. A lot of us like our junk; that is why you sin – because you like your sin; actually it is mostly addiction.

At times it is terrifying to be in the presence of angels. The Bible says that there were angelic visitations and when they appeared it was a terrifying experience.

The Bible says that as Moses was walking around the back of the mountain of Horeb he saw a bush burning, and the angel of the Lord was in the bush. The miracle was not that the bush was on fire, because this happens in Israel. The miracle was that it was burning and the bush was not being burnt up. And so it says that Moses turned aside and that YHVH was in the bush. Moses was not terrified, but there was a desire and a curiosity to know what this thing was. That is one of the things that needs to happen around our lives. We need to develop a holy curiosity. Who are the angels? What is their role and function? How do I relate with them? What do I do?

Angels are holy. The implication in holy is fully aware of the magnitude of the magnificence of YHVH. That awareness of the magnificence of the Father makes them holy because they are continually aware of it. You and I are different because we are not always aware of it, because we live in a fallen body that is sinful.

We are not always aware of the magnificence of the Father. We sometimes lose sight of it, and when we do, the fallen nature begins to rule because you are not in the light. Angels will only be in the light, unless they are fallen angels, so the greater you display the light the greater they are able to abide and the greater the canopy that goes on around your life.

The word 'holy' is a really interesting word when you look at it in the Hebrew. The cherubim were over the ark of God, and the Bible says they cry, "*holy, holy, holy*" (Isaiah 6:3). What they do is they release their wings because of the revelation of what is coming off the ark of God that gets reflected off the nine stones that are over their body. That gets reflected off the gold that their body is made of and releases the realm of the glory into the atmosphere. So what is on them becomes a multi-coloured trans-dimensional thing that gets released into the atmosphere. The word holy means, "Wow! Awesome! Amazing! Did you see that? Whoa, the revelation! Whoa, there is no word that can describe it!" It does not mean being blessed by the priest. Holy means being in awe of the revelation knowledge, and the administration of the right of that knowledge. It means being in awe of the revelation knowledge, because you and I are supposed to receive revelation from the throne of the Father into our lives so that we can administrate revelation, not just knowledge. Wisdom and understanding without the revelation knowledge of God is devilish. Ezekiel 28 talks about satan, who is wise, had understanding, but he did not have the revelation knowledge of YHVH in him, but instead violence was found in him.

Angels are strong, they excel in strength, "*Whereas angels, who are greater in power and might, do not bring a reviling accusation against them before the Lord*" (2 Peter 2:11).

Often when angels turn up and we are not aware of them, they are cloaked in a realm that we cannot engage. There are times when they will appear in this world, especially when there is an assignment that YHVH wants to deliver through you or to you. They will turn up and they will often be white. They will not necessarily be nice, small, meek little things. Angels are not weak little beings that we think look like us. There are some that look like us that are known as the Elohim. They look like a man. They are about our size, but they are the only ones. The rest are bigger. I have not even talked about the living creatures yet. I am just talking about angels. Angels are big! I have seen one that was five stories high with wings that would fill a meeting hall and a sword you would not want to get in the way of. They are not weak little things, and they are there for one purpose, to help you in your walk with YHVH. We need to begin to get excited about the revelation that YHVH is releasing about the angelic. The church does not teach it; it has been afraid to because demons have preoccupied the church's thought life. If we have been so preoccupied with demons, or we are so bound by them, we will not want to engage with the truth that angels are there, provided by YHVH, for the administration of His Kingdom around our lives. We are on the face of this earth to be administrators of His Kingdom, not just to be Christians. To just be a Christian means you have just got fire insurance, but He is not lord of your life yet. That means you are just busy doing your own thing. Angels are ministering spirits that are there because YHVH wants to release His kingdom through us. The Kingdom is full of angels.

Angels are clothed in white raiment, *"…Seven angels having the seven plagues, clothed in pure bright linen…"* (Revelation 15:6). Angels sometimes look extremely white, light, radiant, or blue light because blue light is actually gold light. Light reflected through pure gold turns blue but it is a deep, bright, light blue. That is why the sky is bright blue because there is more gold in the atmosphere than on the face of the earth. Angels are clothed in white raiment and are generally light or white or bright (Rev 15:1-4), so not all angels have the appearance of white light. There are some that look like stone, like crystal granite; there are some that have the appearance of a man; there are some that are really tall and huge and some that are small. There are angels that have the same structure as us; they do not have wings on them, they have the same kind of body configuration and they look like us, but they are not like us because they do not have the body limitation on them.

The whole angelic world is really different from the physical world because everything we see in the physical has one structure and one record of DNA. We all look the same, although we might be different colours, shapes, sizes, male and female. We all generally have two arms, two legs, a head, ears, eyes, nose, mouth, hands, feet, stomach and all the physical features of a human being. The angelic world has a similar appearance but does not necessarily have the same form. Some angels are like characters in the film "The Fantastic Four" – they look like block men. They are made of granite and they look like stone or a kind of crystal. It is the glory of the Lord out of the River of God that they are made out of and the desire and the voice of YHVH; they are created to watch over things.

When they are before the presence of the Lord they become clear and transparent because they are revealed in the glory of YHVH. When we see them, if they are on assignment they often carry a different appearance. When they are around the glory of God, worshiping around the throne, they carry a different appearance. So there are all these different dimensional realm things that are associated with the angelic world that are just amazing. The thing I love about it is that the whole angelic realm is never far away. The reason we think it is far away is because we have been taught that this world we live in right here is so filled with devils that it is only the demonic world that lives here. I have got some really bad news for you: there is a kingdom that has light in it and dark in it and it is all the same kingdom. Part of it has a usurper that lives in it. It should be light, but it is a kingdom in darkness, not a kingdom born of darkness. It is our job to engage the light so that the light can shine and displace darkness.

The Angel of the Lord

I have become fascinated with the angel of the Lord because of the way it opens the door. In the Bible the angel of the Lord is the doorway for the manifestation of the person of YHVH, because it is a sentient being and it often turns up whenever the actual presence of God is going to engage and communicate with man. The angel of the Lord is often a pre-cursor to the appearing of the Father.

The angel of the Lord ministered to Hagar and Ishmael, *"And*

God heard the voice of the lad. Then the angel of God called to Hagar out of heaven, and said to her, "What ails you, Hagar? Fear not, for God has heard the voice of the lad where he is" (Genesis 21:17). The angel of the Lord is a ruler, a governor and a sentient being that is an administrator of the person of YHVH's desire to open the door so that the Father can turn up in a meeting.

I wanted to understand the appearing of the Father, so I began to set my heart to engage Him, which led to an encounter with the angel of the Lord. We were in a meeting when the angel of the Lord showed up in the back of the room as this door of fire opened up. Then the Father came walking into this meeting and the people at the back of the room started screaming! These were people who were spiritual, who had been going to church for years and thought they knew Jesus. The Father turned up in the meeting and there was a radius of about ten or fifteen metres around Him where people were on their faces, under the chairs, screaming, trying to cope with the measure of the presence of YHVH manifesting inside the room because of the angel of the Lord.

The angel of the Lord appeared to Moses in the burning bush and, *"YHVH said to Moses, "I Am Who I Am"; and He said, "You shall say this to the Israelites, 'I Am has sent me to you"* (Exodus 3:14 AMP). The Angel of the Lord moved in a pillar of cloud and the Lord looked through the pillar. Balaam saw the angel of the Lord with a drawn sword. Sometimes YHVH has a real sense of humour. Can you imagine Balaam beating his donkey and there is the angel of the Lord standing in front of the donkey and the donkey turns around and says, "Oy, why are you beating me?" It must have absolutely freaked Balaam out. But the weird thing was that he answered the donkey! I really love going to scripture and trying to figure out how that happened. Because it was almost like it was normal for him to talk to his donkey. I do not think he realised his donkey was speaking back to him.

We have a Kingdom that the Father wants to release that is very important for us and that is why we are here. We are not here just to have a nice Christian life, or do our own thing during the week and come to church on Sunday and call ourselves Christians. Being called Christian means you are supposed to carry the anointing.

That is where the word Christian comes from – Christos, which means the anointed ones. The anointed ones means they had power.

There is an African guy who is almost seven feet tall. He used to be a sorcerer and the way he got his sorcerer garment, or mantle, was to put his hand into a fire and burn his three fingers off. He is now a believer. He got converted, because Jesus showed up, like a white ball of light levitating in the air. This brother preaches that we have power, great power! There is great power in the Kingdom that the Father wants to deliver to us – great power! That power is also involved with the angelic realm. It is not just being a Christian and getting your fire insurance by praying the sinner's prayer. It is beginning to live a godly lifestyle that engages the angelic realm around you, and opening yourself up to the Lord to be a living sacrifice, so that they can walk with you into that place of glory.

Here is the greatest thing: when you are in the middle of your sin you have 70,000 angels watching you. So whenever you think you are alone, and doing things that you think that no one can see, there are 70,000 angels around you. And not only that but the Bible also says: *"Therefore we also, since we are surrounded by so great a cloud of witnesses, let us lay aside every weight, and the sin which so easily ensnares us, and let us run with endurance the race that is set before us"* (Hebrews 12:1). A greater cloud means perhaps 100,000 saints who have gone before you, standing around you, watching what you are doing, hoping that you will choose the right thing, to run the race to the glory. So you now have 170,000 beings watching you.

You cannot hide from the spirit realm. You can go anywhere you like and it is as close to you as the air that you breathe. It is not confined to the natural arena. They can walk through walls, and come out of walls, like we are supposed to be doing and Jesus did.

YHVH has delivered us a Kingdom. The Kingdom is full of power, full of majesty and full of government. It is full of authority and full of angels. The Christian walk is not supposed to be serious and dead. YHVH wants us to walk with His presence. The angelic realm is there to empower you to facilitate the Kingdom around your life.

Activation

Father we want to thank You today that You have put at our disposal the angelic kingdom. Father, before it begins to facilitate around us we need to acknowledge that they are there. Today, Lord, we repent for never acknowledging angelic realms, for never even thinking that they are there or acknowledging that You sent them, because that is where they have come from on assignment, out of Your glory. Lord, we repent before others, we repent before you. Father every deaf and dumb, blinding devil that has shut us out of that realm, Lord, we repent for allowing it into our lives. We take responsibility in our DNA for the record of unbelief that has been engendered within us because no one has talked about the angelic kingdom. Father, today I ask that the angelic realm would begin to open up for us as a church, and as a body of people.

Father, begin to release the angelic realm towards us, to administrate and minister for us, and on our behalf. Lord, I ask for angelic visitations to begin to start for the reader. Father, we ask because your Word says we do not have because we do not ask. Lord, today I am asking. Lord, I come with these people, Father, before Your throne, and we ask for an understanding and an unlocking of the angelic arena and the Kingdom. This is part of your Kingdom, this angelic realm. Father, today we want to acknowledge them. Father, I want to acknowledge the angelic realm of the Kingdom of the Father. I want to acknowledge that they are there. I want to welcome their ministry. Father, today I release them on their assignment, for and on behalf of my life to administrate around me; to go before me, to be my rear guard, to be over me and when I enter into the presence of the Father to become a canopy over my life. Father, I ask that within this world the glory of God and the tabernacle that they would build would become the place of Your presence. Lord, we welcome their ministry today. Father, I thank You for the realm of the Kingdom that you have put at our disposal as sons.

Father, if anyone reading this book is unsaved, does not know you or have a relationship with Your presence then I would ask that You would begin to trouble them, that you get around them and begin to release angels around them. Lord, I ask that they would hear the knocking of YHVH and the voice of YHVH knocking on the door of their hearts. Father I ask that You would trouble them. Father Your Word says that no one can come to the Father unless You draw them. I ask, in Your loving kindness and in Your grace and in Your mercy, that You would draw them into the house of the Lord, into the tabernacle of the ecclesia of YHVH. Father, today we give You thanks for Your grace and Your mercy, that in our ignorance we have let much go by the wayside. Father, empower us today, and lead us to this place. Lord, I ask that the angelic realm of the Kingdom of Heaven would be real to the reader, as part of a body of people and as an individual within that body.

Father, go into every household and to every angel of every house and the angel over every marriage scroll and testimony, to the angel over every individual person, the angel over every area within their city, the angel over every street sign, over every corner post, of every church, over every property that is owned. Father, I ask that over every building that has been built, any angel of God that is in the Kingdom realm that has been assigned by the Father, Lord, we release them to administrate and minister today, Lord, within our city, Lord, move into our city today. Lord, as a group of people we open up our city and we say angelic realm come into this city and administrate within this city. Father, we love Your presence and we worship You. We honour You, Lord, as our God and Saviour, our King, our Father, our friend.

Yeshua HaMashia Elokim, Elohim, YHVH, Shalom. In Jesus' name. Amen.

About Ian

Ian Clayton is the founder of Son of Thunder Ministries and passionately pursues a life of understanding and getting to know who the person of YHVH really is.

Ian travels itinerantly by invitation throughout New Zealand, Africa, America, Europe and Asia ministering, teaching, equipping and mandating people to become sons of God.

Ian's heart in founding Son of Thunder is to have an avenue to put strategies and keys into believers' hands to enable them to actively participate in the reality of the realms of God's Kingdom and to experience the empowerment of life as the spirit beings we were created to be.

Ian trains and equips believers to give their lives in a persistent, passionate pursuit of the person of YHVH, enabling them to discover that their lives are about the preparation for oneness and unity with YHVH for the purpose of becoming mandated and authorised ambassadors of His Kingdom. His passion is to reveal to the sons of God the purpose of the power of the attorney of YHVH within them, removing the sense of powerlessness and hopelessness that is often attached to many in the body of Christ when they are confronted with the reality of the spirit world that surrounds them.

www.sonofthunder.org

Published by
Son of Thunder Publications

www.sonofthunderpublications.org

Made in the USA
Coppell, TX
11 October 2020